A World of Scarcities

A WORLD OF SCARCITIES

CRITICAL ISSUES IN PUBLIC POLICY

DAVID NOVICK

with

KURT BLEICKEN
W. E. DEPUY, JR
STANLEY A. HUTCHINS
J. W. NOAH
MARY B. NOVICK

A HALSTED PRESS BOOK

JOHN WILEY & SONS
NEW YORK – TORONTO

*English language edition, except USA and Canada
published by*
Associated Business Programmes Ltd
17 Buckingham Gate, London SW1

Published in the USA and Canada by
Halsted Press, a Division of
John Wiley & Sons Inc
New York

First published 1976

Library of Congress Cataloging in Publication Data

Novick, David.
    A world of scarcities.

    "A Halsted Press Book."
    1. Natural resources.   2. Energy policy.   3. Economic policy.
I. Title.
HC55.N68   1976   333.7   75-42278

ISBN 0-470-15002-5

© David Novick 1976

Printed in Great Britain by The Anchor Press Ltd
Tiptree, Colchester, Essex

Contents

Acknowledgements

Continuing contact with the Office of Emergency Preparedness, Executive Office of the President (now Office of Preparedness, General Services Administration) provided information and occasion for concern about supplies and potential shortages of strategic raw materials over the last twenty years. To the many good men who headed that agency and particularly Lloyd Eno, Secretary, Program Advisory Committee, I owe a long-standing debt.

RAND Corporation, Santa Monica, California was not only my regular employer for many years but also provided the library and office services without which the mechanics of 'getting out' this book would have been most difficult. Probably more important was the opportunity for exchanging ideas and getting criticism from RAND staff, particularly Dr. G. H. Fisher and Dr. Horst Mendershausen.

Dr. John Hogan of RAND provided knowledgable experience about the mysteries of the world of publishing. Without his help, the project might have been abandoned early in its history. Many others, in California, Washington, DC, New York City, New England and London read part or all of the early or final draft materials. I thank all of them.

Mary B. Novick not only wrote the chapter on aluminum but also read and re-read all of the chapters. Her original responsibility had been viewed as editorial and statistical. It wound up being one of quality controller. Our secretary, Mary E. Fischer, did the usual transcribing and typing plus providing unusual cheery words, newspaper clippings and criticism.

As will become apparent, lots of people helped, and in many different ways. There are five names, other than mine, on six of the chapters herein. Those named are the authors, but final responsibility for what has been committed to print is mine.

28 August, 1975   DAVID NOVICK
                                              Chelsea, Vermont,
                                                        USA

Foreword

Critical Issues in Public Policy, the sub-title of this volume, provides the key to the objective sought. The reason is that although *A World of Scarcities* is the subject, we find that the shortage is really in man's ideas and planning rather than the physical limits of the non-renewable resources of our globe.

We hope you will find every page and every new idea interesting. However, since we have not undertaken a mystery novel or a detective story, it seems sensible to share the conclusion, and the reason for it, right now even before you have plowed through the arguments, ideas and propositions developed herein. That conclusion is that because of scarcities, the world economies are all of them in a bad way for the moment. This need not have happened. It can be treated for the short term and cured completely in the long run. That doesn't mean that either treatment or cure is simple or easy. It isn't. But it is possible.

There are finite limits to natural resources. Man, however, is capable of continuously extending these supplies by appropriate application of technology, economics and politics. The story of aluminum shows how this has been done.

The material developed from an unknown at the beginning of this century into the world's number two metal, today. Bauxite and other aluminous clays are in abundant supply. Nonetheless, it took man a long, long time to discover and develop this resource. Private enterprise started the ball rolling but it was government investment both in preparing for World War II and in keeping the military machinery going in Germany, Japan, the United States and the USSR that brought aluminum into its *Wunderkind* status of recent times.

Just as aluminum has made more material available, the introduction of new ways of handling communications—microwave and communication satellite—have sharply reduced material required for overland and underwater cables. New ways of mov-

ing electric power from generator to consumer are in R and
D and may soon substantially reduce the quantities of materials
used to transmit energy.

In sum, as these illustrations demonstrate, it is well within
man's powers to both reduce material demand and increase supply
from the existing stock of natural resources. Unfortunately, it
seems that we only do this well when trying to fill military requirements for anticipated or on-going conflict.

We believe that the same kind of government planning and
spending can be applied to meeting peacetime requirements,
too. Since no country has yet tried to do that, it calls for a
new and different kind of public policy. This book identifies
issues involved in such a change and provides some of the analysis
which we believe must be in today's debate about tomorrow's
world.

Please read on.

DAVID NOVICK

1. Why Talk About Scarcity Now?

Since World War II, surely since 1950, the nations on the earth planet have enjoyed a new era of prosperity. Both Free World and Iron Curtain countries have had more goods *per capita* than ever before. The Third World nations were caught up in the boom, too, although the gains for most of them were less spectacular than those of their industrialized neighbors.

In these two decades we came to view the world as one in which each year's economic increment was piled on top of that of the prior one, with an assured belief that the years ahead would bring ever higher rates of annual increase. We spoke with satisfaction about our 'real' gains. We pointed with admiration and pride to economic growth rates such as Japan's 12 per cent in the 1960s. And, we felt sorry for England because they were averaging only 2 per cent per year on the growth charts. In short, we seemed to have converted economic theory from the 'dismal science' that had its roots in scarcity, to a 'sanguine science' with a cheerful message about a world of plenty.

It is commonplace to date the conversion of this delightful dream into a nightmare to the Yom Kippur War between the Arabs and Israel. It was in October 1973 that the Persian Gulf oil countries announced and put into effect an embargo, followed by price and rationing controls for their output. This intensified the situation for petroleum, although supply and price 'scarcity' problems had been developing for some time not only for oil, but also for a long list of other natural resources.

Even before the 1973–4 energy crunch, the shortage of materials syndrome had characterized the problems of doing business for a year and more. It was an unusual time for, in the absence of war, industry was confronted with an ongoing set of critical shortages of materials which not only affected profitability and productivity, but also, in some instances, threatened the very operation of industrial concerns. Worldwide competition, national economic contracts, international geopolitics, a long history of inadequate investment and inflation, all combined to produce continuing problems of material shortages for industry. Supply strategy and tactics had become dominant elements in the daily continuance of business operations by late 1972 and well into 1974. Although it sounds strange today, as late as September 1974 the president of the National Association of Purchasing Agents in the United States said, 'now it's the buyers who are out on the road visiting vendors. We're running up fat expense accounts so we can assure our companies a steady flow of raw materials.'

The Arab oil embargo and the resulting dramatic escalation in crude oil prices intensified the economic problems of raw materials. Dislocations in transportation, problems in availability of supplies of fuel and energy for industrial operations, and related disturbances in the economy that the embargo induced, made the overall problems of materials availability only somewhat less trying than those of petroleum itself. Materials costs escalated and the apparent effectiveness of the OPEC cartel raised the specter of similar collective action by other materials-producing countries and the possible vulnerability of the countries of the industrialized world, individually or as groups, to such threats.

The oil exporters' success in escalating prices and immensely boosting their balance-of-payments surpluses had focused world attention on cartels and their potential impact on future relationships between consumers and producers of other basic materials. Most of the natural resource countries looked as though they, too, could organize themselves to do business with the industrial world on the suppliers' terms.

The depression has made it clear that this is not to be. OPEC may weather the storm in the long run, but it is our assumption that even this giant among cartels will have to make both price and supply concessions if it wants to survive. Cartels and their role in a world of scarcities is the subject of a later chapter. This reference is simply a reminder that they are one of the factors to be considered in an analysis of natural resource policy issues.

The Boom is Over

It may seem strange to try to enlist people, business and government into doing something to insure adequate supplies of raw materials for a growth economy now (mid-1975). At present, the scarcities seem to be those of the jobs and personal incomes we associate with full employment. The commodity shortages of 1972–4 and concern about exhausting natural resource supplies seem artificial in an economy that is winding down.

If we accept this negative and/or no-growth condition as our way of life in the future, then this book is a waste of everyone's time. However, if we would like to return to an economy that is dynamic and expanding, then there are a number of things that we must start doing now and into the 1980s. That is, if we want to avoid the kinds of materials scarcities that would have brought the early 1970s business boom to a bumping halt, even without an Arab oil embargo or a four-fold price hike by OPEC, we must act now! The oil situation was so dramatic and well publicized that it tended to obscure very similar potential supply-demand relationships regarding numerous other natural resources.

The thesis here is this. Man makes his own problems and man can resolve them. But it takes time. Many kinds of time: first, to recognize the developing situation; second, to identify what really has happened; third, to formulate the remedial action, and finally to set the machinery for change in motion. Most important, there is the time required to carry out the new program, test it, and make essential modifications in its operations. Five to ten years in most cases, even more if we have been long delayed in recognizing the peril potential as has happened in oil.

What we have already been through, are continuing to endure and will have to put up within the oil situation, is the product of a number and variety of failures by both business and government. One was the refusal to take seriously the early warnings of a crisis potential. Although United States Government studies did lay out policy alternatives for increasing supply and reducing demand through conservation measures in 1969, and even in 1972, there was no effort to develop an action program.

Then when the study projections became realities in the autumn of 1973 there was a desire to wish away the difficulties and no recognition of the earthquake-like impact that would follow the change in price and supply conditions. Unfortunately, the world's financial and industrial structure was not designed to deal with such catastrophic stresses. We assumed they occurred only in times of war. We must learn how to deal with wartime stresses on price and supply conditions in a 'peacetime' world, when there are no military forces battering away at one another and the popular will cannot be rallied against a clearly visible enemy.

Such negative statements do not mean that this book is another doomsday message. Its thesis is not the kind we identify originally with Malthus, subsequently to the conservationists and most recently to the ecology and 'save our planet' groups. *Limits to Growth,** *Mankind at the Turning Point,** *In Defence of Economic Growth,*† and related literature for or against economic growth or the possibility of having an expansion of business and living standards in the future, are not addressed individually and by name here. Economic growth is treated as a factor in producing the scarcities of the early 1970s and as a potential victim of scarcities in the 1980s and the following years, unless policy and programs for increasing supply are action items right now.

The thrust is to illuminate major policy issues and to suggest some of the things that must be done about them. The need for information comes first. Since it may not be of general interest, detailed discussion of data is not included here. In brief, let us point out that each country must take the steps necessary to continuously collect and publish the appropriate data on availability of, and demand for, natural resources for its area. The current national and international effort just does not do the job.

It is only with 'best possible' statistics (complete accuracy is not possible) of this kind that both business and government will be able to make plans for the future. And in natural resource planning we are dealing with long-term projections, five to ten years at a minimum, decades when problems such as additional supplies of a selected resource, like water, must be resolved.

Long-range plans must recognize the uncertain conditions of the world and be able to handle the changes that always occur. That calls for flexibility, not rigidity. It also attaches great importance to option preserving and hedging techniques. A good illustration of the need for preserving options is available in man-made artificial fibers based on petroleum. If we had abandoned wool and cotton research in the late 1950s because of the attractions of the newly-available polyesters, we would be in great difficulties now that petroleum has upset the artificial fiber game. Hedging needs are filled by activities such as continued construction of coal and hydro-electric power generating facilities even though it appears that nuclear power will sweep the field, as was the case some ten years ago. We all know where we would be now

---

*Club of Rome Sponsored Books.
† By Wilfred Beckerman, Jonathan Cape (London, 1974).

and for the rest of the century if the atomic power enthusiasts had had their way a while back.

Obviously this is just a proposal that we act prudently and sensibly. In a complex and highly-integrated world economy, this is not an easy accomplishment. Adam Smith's *Economic Man* can hardly do it as an individual. There must be public policy guidance and government action to enable today's enterprises to make effective plans for supplies of the materials essential to their output.

Abundance to Scarcity

Up to now we operated on the assumption that there was an unlimited supply not only of energy but also of all natural resources. This made economic growth a major objective of practically all the countries in the world. Although we tend to overlook it now, the unprecedented prosperity of the years 1970–4, showed that we had reached a point in time when nature's bounty no longer could be taken for granted, and that ideas about economic growth would have to be re-examined. That is, without the appropriate long-range planning, man was making problems and not doing anything about them.

The 1974 energy crisis was only the tip of an iceberg of natural resource supply and demand problems created by the hyper-prosperity that we had been enjoying. The post-World War II phenomenal rates of economic growth had meant using up mineral, timber, fiber and food resources much more rapidly than additional sources of supply were being developed.

One obvious result has been that we were not able to satisfy world-wide demands for energy. Less obvious, but equally important, is the fact that if we were to break that bottleneck and get back to early 1970 growth rates, the increasing scarcity of a number of other non-renewable resources would immediately overtake us. The future situation in other materials can be a mirror image of the recent past in energy.

In the decade just closed, while wealth and living standards were expanding rapidly in the United States, the Common Market countries and Japan (and even faster in some countries that not too long ago were thought to be backward, such as Iran) we neglected the implications and meaning of industry's ever-increasing appetite for fuel and raw materials. We failed to take into our calculations the millions of additonal workers who had moved above the subsistence level and had become active bidders for beef, wool, and automobiles. We must not be guilty of the same kind of short-sightedness this time around.

The demand-induced shortage of energy of the last few years had been lurking in the background for some time. So also were the problems in the demand and supply of aluminum, meat, copper, breadstuffs, cotton and on and on. It is an Arabian Nights' Dream to assume that everything can be set to rights just by having the sheiks drain down their Persian Gulf oil basin. It's another dream to assume that when prosperity is restored we can quickly resolve the threat of another series of basic material scarcities. This means that economic projections for the years up to 1985 must be made in terms of the equitable sharing of shortages. The realities of zero or minus rates of growth will enforce a new concept of national and international development for the next several years. Sometime after 1985 we may be able to return to our 1970–4 life-style.

Emphasis on the next ten years results from recognition of the fact that, ultimately, we will solve the technological and economic problems of growth or demand-induced scarcity. But it takes time to do it. Although money can be used to buy some quantity of time, as it was in developing the atomic bomb and man's roundtrip to the moon, money alone cannot produce 'instant natural resource supply'. In fact, ten years seems a physical and technological minimum even when economic considerations are minimized.

The atom bomb project started in 1940 and a few, difficult-to-handle, devices became available in 1945. It was the mid-1950s before there was 'on-line production' of the items required for large-scale use. In 1961 President Kennedy called for 'a man on the moon in this decade', and we just about managed it. These two technological achievements demonstrate that man can solve his problems given time and willingness to allocate large resources to that future goal instead of today's demands.

The specter of running out of food because of unlimited population growth was raised by Malthus in the eighteenth century. Another British economist, Jevons, had coal supplies exhausted in the 1800s. There was an oil crisis, whale oil, in the middle of the nineteenth century. More than fifty years ago, President 'Teddy' Roosevelt said timber, oil and other materials were limited and that the United States would soon exhaust its supplies of these natural resources. Nonetheless, except during the major demand-supply dislocations in World War I and World War II, most countries have managed to meet all of their requirements up to now.

In late 1973 and early 1974, most economists, financial analysts, government officials and journalists were saying that the petroleum-energy problem would be resolved in short order. Some had it happening in 1974, others in an additional year or two. *The Economist*, a highly respected and authoritative journal not generally known for wild guessing about the future, gave these reasons for optimism at the beginning of 1974:

1. Shortages in a highly developed industrial society result in crash programs for increasing productive capacity. Since 1945, there have been at least fifteen instances in which critical shortages led within a decade to over-production. [They then go on to cite the outstanding cases.]

2. No industry has responded more quickly or fully to financial incentives than the petroleum industry. In the past few years, however, these incentives have been drying up. Now that they are being restored and, indeed, dramatically increased, a lot more people and a lot more investment capital are going to get into the act.

   The sharp increase in the price of oil per barrel will accelerate petroleum exploration and development.

3. Predictions concerning future world oil development are based on past methods for finding oil. New techniques, utilizing electronic sensors and computerized systems, may open up areas not now included in forecasts.

4. Most predictions about the increase in energy needs do not take into account the development of new technology that will require less energy to accomplish the same purposes. The increased use of transistors and miniaturized integrated circuits will do away with millions of tons of machinery now being driven by conventional power. A large electronic church organ, for example, that now requires a ton of operating equipment will be able to make the same music with a miniaturized circuit no larger than a half-dollar and weighing less than half a pound.

That was a more elegant presentation of our 'man can solve his problems'. The 'but it takes time' part of our thesis can be read into its 'within a decade'. When it is, the seeming promise for quick solutions recedes some years further back into the calendar.

That is unless we manage to find a glut of energy right now. *The Economist* did. In its 3 March 1975 issue under 'The North Sea Bubble' heading, they reported: 'Over a year ago *The Economist* unfashionably suggested that there was a "coming glut of energy". Well it's here earlier, earlier than we expected.' The supporting analysis covered Mr. Kissinger's floor price of $7.00 a barrel, redundant capacity at that price in Alaska and North Sea oil, and British and American coal. It reviewed 'the boycott that wasn't', cartel operations in the period before Yom Kippur 1973 and the fact that OPEC optimists say that the drop in demand is caused by world recession. They then come to their key argument: that there is more than enough energy already available and about to come to power the economic recovery, and for there to be energy left over.

With that, the writer forcefully disagrees, because accepting it means commitment to a world economy operating at 5 per cent below early 1970s levels. There is no need to accept a 'poor' economy. The reason for this position is that even though the first and longer quote from *The Economist* is now several years old, very little, in fact practically nothing, has been done by way of crash programs for increasing productive capacity. There has been a bit more done about the Arctic Slope, North Sea and other previously discovered new fields but none of this is on a scale or promises the speedy results we impute to 'crash programs'. There has not yet been anything in the form of the World War II radar and atom projects or the 1960s space undertakings.

This lack of 'quick fix' undertakings in oil is stressed for two reasons: first, as a demonstration of how long it is likely to take to start on other natural resource problems and second, because our current experience should have given us a more meaningful understanding of lead-time–the years from concept to useful output. It takes a long time for natural resource expansion; a decade is a more appropriate measuring stick than a year.

That's why we must be concerned about the shortages that developed in 1970–4. If we get back on the expansion trail, material scarcities will again be roadblocks in the late 1980s. That is, unless we do something about them *now*. Current emphasis is on stimulating consumption to turn the business curve up again. That makes it difficult to reconstruct 1973 demand-induced recession–reduced economic activity due to industry's inability to deliver goods because of material shortages.

The demand recession faded into the over-supply depression in 1974. Business had stopped growing in 1973 and by October 1974 the direction of the output curves for automobiles, housing and other consumer durables had gone into reverse. That cut down industry's requirements for aluminum, copper, iron, timber and other basic materials. (The inventory boom that covered up the worst of the business picture until October 1974 will be discussed later.)

Depression is an unpleasant way to deal with materials scarcities. However, if we have not done anything to increase supplies of these raw materials by the time more energy becomes available in the 1980s, we will suddenly find we are again short of many of the other materials that are the basic building blocks of modern prosperity. So, we must try to learn to do something that we do not like to do, that is, plan for the future before the crisis is upon us.

Up to now, government planning by industrialized countries has been concerned largely, almost entirely, with problems of demand. Policy decisions were based on expenditure surveys, program budgets and plans. The tools for carrying out policy determinations were up and down movements in government spending, taxing, borrowing, the rediscount or bank rate and the money aggregates. Although the staff documents were prepared in terms of dates five or ten years into the future, decisions and actions were essentially short term.

That was the essence of our future planning. It is easy to understand how natural resource supply problems that take five, ten or more years to handle found no home, no one to take responsibility for them in that planning context. For that reason, when petroleum and other natural resource shortages started to show up in the early 1970s, no one was willing or able to do anything about them.

There was just no way to handle physical limitation on supply in our current concept of economic management through monetary and fiscal policy. The Keynesian approach put the emphasis on managing demand. To stimulate a lagging economy, government prods demand by stepping up its own spending or by placing more money in the hands of individuals or corporations, or both.

The early 1970s saw that government stimulation could make demand outrun supply. During that period, as a result, there was a world-wide boom, something that rarely happens. Facilities were straining at capacity and beyond. And major shortages of materials were popping up. Since we were continually in fear that the unprecedented economic growth would flatten out, we tried new monetary or fiscal stimuli, or some combination of them, to stay on the upswing. In the United States, the Federal Reserve Board, the Administration and Congress each took turns trying to forestall a downturn. When the energy scarcity crystallized the picture, it became clear that we had reached a point where pump priming meant that the pump could only spit out more inflation. So we tried financial restraint first, but not for long. Since inflation is more popular than recession, the minute there was any doubt about the future we went back to the more-money method to stimulate the economy.

Evaluating time, economic, political and environmental constraints in formulating public policy is difficult even when we can use money as a common denominator in describing multi-varied situations. Now we cannot generalize in terms of budget or economic dollars alone, but must instead learn how to do our planning and policy-making subject to physical constraints – energy and other natural resources. In doing this we must distinguish between the short haul and the long one; between a depressed economy and a growing one. If we manage to turn the business curve up again for the next five years energy will be short. If we manage to get back to a 4 per cent per annum or higher economic growth rate in the United States by 1985 (that means there is enough energy to do it) all natural resources other than those needed for energy will be scarce.

If the energy shortage is real, and we think it is, our 1930s anti-depression steps just will not do the job. Public works, housing, low-cost loans to business and industry, all of these produce added energy requirements. First, for transportation and fabrication of the equipment needed to create the buildings and machinery, and later, for the operation and use of them. So, without additional supplies of energy, we will have to go back to leaf-raking, paper-pushing and other white- and blue-collar projects powered by humans rather than the gasoline or electrical energy we are now accustomed to use.

At this point, the energy shortage for an expanding economy overshadows and postpones problems of other natural resource scarcities. In this discussion we look beyond the economic valley and into the rising slopes of prosperity of the late 1980s. We hope by then the world will have escaped from the grip of the energy problem and again be in a position to enjoy significant economic growth. In developing this picture we will refer to the shortages in the currently available supplies of natural resources that appeared in the early 1970s.

Those scarcities developed because our satisfaction with prosperity was so complete that we failed to recognize the danger signals in the explosive rates of growth in *per capita* and total demand for practically everything that had been taking place. We must not permit that to happen again.

Appropriate public policy to rectify this condition will be both costly and irksome, but we can develop one that will prop up the economy now and provide an effective base for future growth. The significant issues for this kind of discussion are set out in the next chapter. The experience of the United States is used in this discussion not only because that is the one I am most acquainted with, but also because the United States consumes somewhere between 30 and 45 per cent of available world supplies of natural resources (depending on whose calculations are used). This means that United States policy must play a prominent role in the deliberations of all other countries and is not just misplaced emphasis on my part.

The experience of the United States will be used also in a discussion in Chapter 3 of developing issues for policy debates on energy. Petroleum and its OPEC cartel are prominent in any energy discussion and suggests the brief overview of other potential natural resource cartels (Chapter 4). We turn then to a discussion of the most critical basic materials starting with aluminum and fertilizers and running through timber and on to zinc. These demand-supply analyses are each presented separately in the Selected Natural Resources Appendix. Chapter 5 draws off the highlights of that presentation as a prelude to a discussion of the public policy determinations that we deem essential. Chapter 6 is a continuation of the ideas introduced in Chapters 2 and 3, as well as the conclusion which sets out our ideas on meaningful policy and programs for implementing it.

2. Natural Resource Issues for Public Policy

Through the amazing development of applied technology over the last two centuries, we seemed to have achieved a complete domination of nature. But our new tools became powerless during the energy crisis and by that time petroleum was only one of the natural resources whose scarcity had started to challenge man's supremacy in the struggle with nature. In a few years, the United States has gone from being a surplus holder in energy, and a number of other raw materials, to a deficit nation. Other industrialized countries such as Japan, with very limited natural resources, found themselves in a desperate scramble for energy and other commodities.

We do not know what the final outcome of this new struggle over natural resources will be in terms of international power balance and economic rivalry. We do know that for the next decade the industrialized world can no longer make plans based on larger supplies of raw materials, or even the quantities that it consumed in the past. The comfortable days are over, and we must now formulate public policy so as to maximize welfare under entirely new conditions.

The issues involved raise tremendous questions that the citizens of the industrial countries of the world must prepare themselves to answer. One reason why so many honestly believe they have the solution to the scarcities scare is that they do not really believe there is a problem. Nonetheless, unless we can cut demand for the short run and increase supply in the long run, the industrial countries face a series of depressing situations including inadequate materials for a growth economy, vulnerability to acts of foreign suppliers and the return of the boom-and-bust business cycle.

Probably the first course of action is to develop the goals of a materials policy and state them in terms everyone can understand. The overall goal requires programs for reducing demand as well as increasing supply expressed in quantities and time schedules. This will require a comprehensive natural resources materials policy that includes the following:

1. Reduce demand by conservation, substitution and new technology.
2. Increase supply by exploration, investment and new technology.
3. Prepare for emergencies.
4. Determine the management method–business or government or appropriate combination.

In formulating the policy alternatives we must be actively aware of two major time contexts: one, the more remote period in which we hope to realize the fruit of our new directions; and the other, the immediate years ahead when action must be initiated if the sought-for results are to be possible of achievement at the desired time.

Let us start with the second time dimension. This is essential because whether we are looking at 1985, 2000 or beyond, the policies and programs we adopt for natural resources in the next two or three years will determine whether we can again support a growth economy twenty or thirty years from now.

Saying 'twenty or thirty years from now' may be both surprising and disappointing. Nonetheless, if we are realistic and review the time it takes to carry out each part of the program required to deal with natural resource scarcities, it is clear that for the decade immediately ahead only small additions to supply are possible. Some meaningful expansion can be achieved over the next ten years, but it is only by 1995 and beyond that real improvement in the quantities available is possible.

Let us remind ourselves that before we start to dig new pits or mines or to build new smelters and refineries, a number of geological, technical, financial and political questions must be resolved. These include: where is the natural resource located, by what methods can it be extracted and processed, what will it cost, and what is its business value at current or likely future prices? Then come the questions of government involvement such as financial support, environmental control, international relationships and other policy issues. First of all it is necessary to discuss the lead-time problems facing us since they make immediate action vital.

Lead-time

Time required from origin of the request to its fulfilment is called lead-time. Energy is used as the illustration because it has been the center of discussion for some time and its technical, transportation, labor and related requirements are much the same as those to be met for other natural resource materials.

The lead-time in an energy expansion program in the United States takes several forms: (i) specialized equipment such as turbines and generators; (ii) materials, particularly alloy steel plate and tubing; (iii) labor demands ranging from equipment operators, welders and other trades on up into a variety of engineering-degree skills; (iv) transportation, such as new pipelines for oil or gas, and railroads or highways for new coal fields; and (v) availability of large-scale contractors of the size of Bechtel, Knudsen, etc. If the supply of any of these is inadequate, a process of picking and choosing is required to determine how the limited resources that are available are to be allocated.

Furthermore, the determination of priority among the projects will not be a one-off action but a continuing and changing one. Among the reasons for this, probably the most important one, is lead-time or the number of months or years required to produce the items in short supply.

For labor skills: The organized labor time to accreditation ranges from eighteen months to five years; college-trained engineers are a four-year plus situation; and moving workmen from surplus areas to places where they are needed also takes inducements, careful scheduling and time measured in years.

For materials like alloy steel plates and tubing, normal deliveries are around one year even if capacity is adequate. When additional facilities must be provided, then two or three more years are involved. *Turbines* are a two-or-more-years item at best. Multiply that time by four and more if new capacity must be created.

Adding new contractors who can handle large-scale projects is largely a question of competition for existing specialities when the energy contracts are to be let. Developing new ones and establishing their reliability takes a very long time.

Any time any of these categories—critical products, critical materials, critical labor or management skills—are in short supply, some kind of resource allocation will need to be considered. How and whether it will have to be invoked depends on the magnitude of the resource demand in the programs for which preferred treatment may have to be sought.

Increased supply is a vital part of the solution to the scarcities problem. But we cannot wish away the problems of time and money. Even conventional energy sources have a longer lead-time than most of us realize. It takes at least five years to locate and bring offshore oil sources to production, ten years to get a nuclear power plant into operation, the same or more years to open up new coal fields. Exotic new sources, such as solar energy, are many years away.

Although memories of the years of prosperity just past might lead us to assume we can do anything we want to do and do it quickly, it would be foolish to delude ourselves with that idea. Lead-time considerations will have to be included in the public policy debate as well as be an important part of the determinations it produces.

PUBLIC POLICY ISSUES ON THE DEMAND SIDE

While demand for natural resources has been exploding in recent years, lead-time, price, environment and political considerations have precluded the same kind of change in the supply of them. Since we have yet to do even the essential planning on the supply side, it means that, for the next decade, practically everything we can expect to accomplish will have to be done in terms of demand. This means not only cutting back on 1973 rates of use but also cutting back even more than we would like.

A deep cut is necessary to make possible the investment in projects for expanding future production. The National Academy of Engineering has estimated the *direct* investment for the United States Project Independence at $700 billion. Other calculations put the full cost at $2 trillion including infrastructure for energy alone. If the same policy was applied to the other natural resource problems, it is easy to see that we quickly run up a total of something like $2–$3 trillions in 1973 dollars.

Even with the United States gross national product at $1.5 trillion a year, it is clear that investments of the magnitude just mentioned can be accomplished only by reducing current consumption. Never before have we seen a problem of such scale, involving such imponderables–monetary, economic, social, technological and political.

There are a number of reasons for the industrial world's slowness in coming to grips with the scarcity problems, in petroleum and other natural resources. The overriding one, as we see it, is that the task is one of redesigning the world to fit this new situation. When we recognize that, and put it in terms of the next ten years, we have to swallow a really bitter pill–reducing our standard of living. And this time there is no war, no visible enemy responsible for the cut. There is, instead, the lesson we should have learned from petroleum. That is, that it takes continuous analysis, forethought, planning and time to deal with our problems. In short, we should continually work at our problems instead of waiting until major dislocations force action.

Conservation, Substitution and New Technology

1. Conservation. Conservation has great potential and promise for cutting down demand because most products now in use were designed with the philosophy that materials are abundant and cheap. Equally, or more important, is the fact that a meaningful program for saving material keeps money in the customers' pockets. Since natural resources have been easy to come by and the least costly of the factors of production, in the past there was no incentive for either original product design or subsequent redesign to stress commodity savings. For a long time, major emphasis has been on labor saving, and this meant not only more and better machinery but also more wasteful use of material. This appeared in many ways, most notably through over-specification and throw-away instead of repair.

Designs requiring larger quantities and/or higher quality material than minimum standards would call for, were intended to avoid breakdown or rework in the factory, and reject and return by the buyer. It was simpler to overspecify in terms of quality, quantity or both and pay the relatively small sums involved, than to incur the much higher cost for disrupting production, or deteriorating relationships with customers. As a result of the change in price and availability of many basic materials, at current prices there is a tremendous opportunity for conservation of natural resources in practically every product in everyday use. An illustration of what we can do to conserve is a greater concentration of soup in a can. The smaller can saves not only tin and steel in tinplate but also paperboard in cartons, and cubic feet of space on store shelves, warehouses and trucking. It also means more cans per shipping container, more cartons per truck, and fewer handlers all along the line. There are numerous other possibilities for this kind of conservation.

Consumption habits also developed in terms of the idea that materials are cheap. The modern concept of convenience was based on disposal instead of re-use. The widespread substitution of disposable plastic or paper products for ones formerly made of cloth or ceramic is typical. For the housewife, it is a question of alternate uses of her time, for example, hours saved, or so she can earn a second income for the family. For the employer it's a labor and cost trade-off, well demonstrated by the use of paper or plastic in cafeterias and convenience food shops to replace dish washing.

In the same fashion, when a gadget breaks down it is simpler to throw it away. This may be the result of more attractive designs or advertised better performance of the current models. Or, it frequently means that the product's original design does not permit repair. That is the so-called 'designed obsolescence' which consumer organizations have long complained about.

Whatever the reason, both consumers and producers have habits of making and using objects that place materials conservation at the bottom of the list of economic considerations. If there is any problem in visualizing what is meant just think of the gasoline-guzzling automobiles of 200 horsepower and higher.

So, we have a large store of bad practices on which to draw as well as a clean slate on which to start writing our conservation rules.

2. Substitution. Substitution can take a number of forms. We can replace the present activity with an entirely new one in which the kinds and quantities of materials used are drastically revised. These include for example, walking to work or to the library instead of driving solo in a 200 h.p. car; re-use of old material instead of new, which made possible the old-time junk or now familiar re-cycling activities; or the substitution of a less scarce material for one in tight supply. Each of these will be developed more fully in the next paragraphs.

Historically, growth or improved well-being meant not only satisfying old wants but adding to the list of goods considered necessities. This trend has had a marked impact on the way in which we used natural resources for a century or more, and has been particularly pronounced since 1960. Only wars or depressions have caused us to reduce consumption of materials by substituting new conditions, such as cold and dark homes for the then preferred warm and bright ones a growing economy had made possible. We did this in times of war for patriotic or government regulation reasons. We did it in times of depression to conserve personal funds. Whatever the reason, it was a substitution of a new condition in order to conserve natural resources.

The re-use of old material can take place in a number of forms including salvage, rework or recycling. Salvage takes carburetors, hub caps and other parts from 'junk' autos and uses them for replacements. The concept extends through a variety of reclaiming activities including the working of tailings from mineral deposits and the recovery of sunken cargo.

Many materials that can no longer be used for their original design purpose can be reworked into materials to be used for another purpose. For example, when old railroad tracks can no longer pass inspection on right-of-way use, they can be re-rolled into reinforcing bars for concrete construction.

Recycling is turning old newspapers into paper and paperboard, used cans into metal, and non-returnable bottles into new ceramic materials. Although not a conversion process, using 'deposit' bottles over and over again for the identical use is the epitome of recycling.

A dramatic picture of material re-use is provided by automobiles. Around 90 per cent of the cars taken out of service are recycled for their material content. In the United States about 4 million of the scrapped vehicles have been processed by some hundred auto-shredders each year. A shredder is a giant hammer mill machine that takes a complete car and reduces it to fist size fragments. This output is divided into three categories: one goes to steel mills and foundries; another goes to plants that recover non-ferrous metals; and the third which is being used chiefly for land fill. Much of that which currently is land fill, is plastics and polymers. Retrieving re-use material from these current land fill candidates is being researched and looks promising.*

Substituting a cheaper or more easily workable material for the one traditionally used has long been the *forte* of some alert manufacturers. Using labor instead of material when it was the cheaper factor of production has also been an entrepreneurial approach. Many industrial-world readers will find it difficult to think the second case is possible. I suggest that they examine the abundant trade-union and manufacturing-association literature seeking government intervention against the 'flood of slave-made goods'. These pleas have come from one country after another, as it has passed over the dividing line between developing and industrialized nations.

Wherever labor is plentiful and cheap, the opportunity to trade off labor for material arises. A representative case is that of the Japanese cotton cloth industry prior to World War II. Since labor was their low cost item, they produced finished cloth that was cheaper by the yard but more expensive by the pound.

---

*In 1975, England's Wolfson Foundation made a £60,000 grant for such research to the University of Liverpool.

This was done by spinning finer yarns and then weaving them into standard constructions like an 80 square shirting which measured and looked like the British or American made but weighed less per square yard. More spinning uses less raw cotton and more hours of work. Similar practices are found today in Hong Kong, Singapore and India for example.

Realization of the neo-Malthusian thesis could put much, if not all, of the world back into that same kind of desperate scramble for a livelihood. When food and all other natural resources are in short supply *vis-à-vis* population, there would be a universal tendency to substitute labor for materials.

For the world of scarcity, we envisage substituting a more plentiful material for one in short supply as a more meaningful approach. Here, we must take care that we have full knowledge of the potential ramifications of what can happen. In World War II, when we mandated wood as a substitute for steel in the United States, the final result was to substitute one critical shortage for another as is described below.

In 1942–3, the most critical shortages seemed to be aluminum, copper, rubber and steel. Substitutes and replacements were searched for intensively. For example, silver from the Government Reserve at Fort Garrison was turned into buss bars for the Tennessee Valley Authority's power system so that the copper ·ones they replaced would be used as additions to wartime supply. In the scramble for substitution there was a suggestion for wooden airplanes, (Howard Hughes built the 'Spruce Goose', a long-range bomber), wooden ships, but the important substitution that was put into force was replacing lumber for steel in most building applications.

Since all construction was under specific authorization, it appeared that the structural demand could be controlled and substantial quantities of iron and steel shifted into other purposes. Unfortunately, no one had calculated the crating and packing requirements for lumber in an overseas war. That demand turned out to be astronomical. As a result, by late 1943–4, we were substituting steel for lumber in construction since timber had become the more critical shortage.

The reverse of this situation occurred in alloy steels. Because nickel and other alloy materials are essential, not only for finished military equipment, but also in the machinery for manufacturing them, this problem reached the critical stage in the United States even before Pearl Harbor. After a number of studies and conferences, a series of national emergency specifications that reduced quantities for the alloys in shortest supply and increased amounts for the ones more readily available were made mandatory. Despite sincere warnings that the shifts would result in equipment below military standards and therefore, spelled catastrophe, it did work. In fact, it worked so well that, with the end of hostilities, the national emergency label was dropped and in many uses they became standard specifications.

3. New technology. New technology will ultimately provide the substitution, conservation and reclaiming processes that will reduce new requirements for natural resources. But, here we come back again to the lead-time problem. In the absence of The Three Princes of Serendip, unless research has already advanced to the development, test and evaluation stage, the sought-for benefits are at least ten years away. And up to now, most of the research and development in materials has aimed at environmental considerations rather than materials savings. In fact, in many cases, natural resource requirements have been increased, for example by reducing auto emissions.

To be sure the more demanding automobile emission standards did lead into weight-savings studies as a means for offsetting decreased miles per gallon caused by the devices introduced to reduce air pollution. There has always been a search for new materials and new processes, but at the commodity prices that prevailed up to 1970 there was little drive behind this search. Even with the 1974 petroleum emergency, ideas about secondary and tertiary recovery, liquification or gasification of coal or shale, geo-thermal and solar sources make the headlines but little else. There has been some talk but very little funding of the research and development that must be done first.

New technology in natural resources means much more than oil and gas. We need to reduce the quantity of virgin materials needed not only for original design, but also for processing activities, machining, scrap and waste. The rich output of the research and development expansion that has become available since 1940 gives us reason for faith in technology. There is potential for solving our problems, but first we must work at them. Once again, we must remind ourselves of the lead-time required which means starting to make the investment required right now.

PUBLIC POLICY ISSUES ON THE SUPPLY SIDE

Lead-time, time to act, money and investment were expressions used repeatedly in our discussion of public policy for the demand side of the natural resources problems. They also will be prominent in our examination of questions that must be resolved in establishing public policy for supply.

Probably the first issue for analysis is the way in which a country should handle its relationship with its external or foreign sources. For countries that depend largely on outsiders (for example, England and Japan import practically all of their supplies of most materials that are likely to be scarce) this is a very tricky issue. Stockpile, ownership of foreign mines, smelters, political control of major foreign sources, long-term contracts with foreign sellers are some of the possibilities that immediately come to mind in thinking about assuring a steady supply. Then the next thing that comes to mind is that, except for stockpiling, it is obvious that each one of the other approaches involves risks such as price escalation, interruption of movement by seizure, embargo, blockade, war or just downright orneriness.

For countries that have substantial natural resource endowments such as the United States, the situation is slightly different. Nonetheless, in 1970 the United States imported all of its primary supplies of chromite, columbium, mica, rutile, tantalum and tin; more than 90 per cent of its antimony, bauxite, cobalt, manganese and platinum; more than half of its asbestos, beryl, cadmium, fluorspar, nickel, and zinc; and more than a third of its iron ore, lead and mercury'.* Although the situation becomes less intense as we move down the percentage reliance on imports scale, interruption of supply or a sky-rocketing price situation in any of these materials will cause real damage to the domestic economy.

After we have a good understanding of what is involved in relying on imports, we can then start to establish quantity and time objectives for the expansion of internally-held supplies through stockpiles, increased domestic production or a combination of both. In large measure, the materials' supply goals will be a function of national economic growth objectives tempered by the reality of world prosperity and depression, population growth rates, and degree of stability in the relationships between nations. Once the goals for growth have been set, we can then turn to the management method available for carrying out the programs involved.

Several of the issues mentioned above will be examined more fully in the following pages.

---

* *Materials and Man's Needs*, National Academy of Sciences, Washington, DC (1974).

Dependence on Foreign Sources

No country in the world is completely self sufficient through its natural endowments of non-renewable resources. Brazil, China, the United States, and the USSR, come close but each one depends on outsiders for all or part of its requirements for each one of a significant list of materials that are critical to its well-being. For example, Brazil must import most of its petroleum.

The quotation from *Materials and Man's Needs* capsulizes the American situation. It ranges from 100 per cent imports for chromite and some others; 90 per cent foreign supplies of anti-mony, etc., half of the asbestos and a third of others such as iron ore. Although the United States could manage to survive without these materials, it would be quite a different country if the terms of trade in any one of them were changed drastically.

In short, doing without or becoming independent of foreign sources both involve prohibitive social, political and economic costs. If we are in reality denied autarky, what do we do? The simple context would be to return to the classical economists' 'free trade' based on comparative advantage.* However, our long history of trade disrupted by war and our current experience with supply manipulation and sky-rocketing price for oil make us hesitant about that approach. We want protection against the risk of catastrophic change which would threaten or overtake us in peace or war.

That means stockpiling as well as research and development of alternative materials and conservation. The issue is how to reduce the dangers when materials become scarce, without con-verting the effort into a world-wide economic plague. There seems to be universal agreement that the world permitted itself to be too dependent on current imports of oil; petroleum buffer stocks are an imperative; and OPEC management has been an economic catastrophe for developing and developed countries. So, how far

---

*David Ricardo developed the concept of comparative advantage as the basis for international trade. His illustration on the exchange of cloth from England for wine from Portugal was 'England may be so circumstanced that to produce the cloth may require the labour of 100 men for one year; and if she attempted to make the wine, it might require the labour of 120 men for the same time. England would therefore find it her interest to import wine, and to purchase it by exporting of cloth.' This is quoted here simply to try to avoid the confusion between absolute and relative advan-tage. Although not international trade, the idea may be even better demonstrated in Ricardo's 'Two men can both make shoes and hats, and one is superior to the other in both employments; but in making hats he can only exceed his competitor by one-fifth or twenty per cent, and in making shoes he can excel him by one-third or 33 per cent—will it not be for the interest of both that the superior man should employ himself exclusively in making shoes and the inferior man in making hats.' That is for each one to employ his comparative advantage.

do we want to go in being independent in materials? How far should we go? How far can we go in the long run? In the short run?

Stockpiling Supply

Although there is a substantial history of stockpiling materials for war purposes, for example, Nazi Germany in the 1930s and the United States since 1940, there has been relatively little use of this method for economic stability reasons. Only with the material supply and price problems that developed in 1971 and 1972 was serious attention given to normalizing peace time supply for consumers through buffer stocks. Producer cartels have a long history of attempts to use buffers (*see* Chapter 4).

Since 1971 England, France, Japan, Sweden, the United States and West Germany all voiced interest in consumer protection through buffer stocks, the idea being to insure continuity of supply and to maintain changes of prices at realistic levels. However, only Japan took action.* In 1972 they established an $800 million fund to buy materials whose scarcity was threatening the Japanese economy. Subsequently, as prices slipped and energy created balance-of-payment problems, Japan became a seller from its hoards most notably in copper, zinc and timber.

This is not the first time that buffer stocks were not used for their original purpose. The Stevenson Plan for crude rubber fell apart in the mid-1920s and the cartel then dumped its stocks into an already depressed market. The experience was the same for a number of other price support cartels during the great depression as well as post World War II co-operative efforts to support prices in coffee and some other commodities. The historic experience has been almost entirely with producer price support.

There were at least two theoretic works on economic stabilization through stockpiling, one by Benjamin Graham, a noted financial analyst.† He proposed an International Corporation of Governments to operate a stockpile for both material consuming and producing countries. Its objective was to keep price fluctuations within fixed ranges and by this means to minimize business cycle swings. That proposal was printed in 1944.

In 1952, another stockpile for economic stability was suggested

---

*The United States Budget for FY 1976 included a proposal for a two billion board feet timber stockpile.

†Benjamin Graham, *World Commodities and World Currencies*, McGraw-Hill (New York, 1944). In its original version, *Storage and Stability*, McGraw-Hill (New York, 1937), Graham advocated a multi-commodity standard for national currencies. *Money and the Mechanism of Exchange*, W. S. Jevons suggested the same concept in 1875.

by Grondona.* It differed from Graham in two basic concepts: first, it was a private corporation, and second, its policy and programs were rigid and expressed in a mandatory buy-and-sell formula. Thus, the idea of buffering economic swings in material price and availability is not a brand new one, although neither Graham's nor Grondona's ideas got beyond the book stage. In the past, cartel stockpiles have been abandoned and Japan's recent stocking actions have not produced results that looked promising. None of this should stop us from taking a fresh new look at either available theory or active experience.

The concept deserves a new look because there is so much at stake in the material scarcity problem. Its impact is felt in terms of international relations and the economic condition of both the total world and individual countries.

Analysis of stockpile proposals must consider very early the forms and shapes, as well as the condition, of the material to be held in stock. Should it be raw, processed, or in a primary form like ingots? If raw, should it be ready to ship or just readily available? Obviously, the more the inventory approximates regular trade practice the more easily it can be used by industry. However, if the stockpile is to represent as much as one, two or more years of calculated requirements, there may be ecological, economic or political reasons to move further up or down the processing road than is the current practice.

Part of the decision on form and condition may be the result of cost considerations. To establish a stockpile, numerous costs direct and indirect, one-time investment plus recurring annual expenses, must be incurred. Even the seemingly easy-to-estimate outlays can prove to be complicated. This is due to uncertainties with respect to the quantity, time and price at which the material will move into or out of stocks.

Then there will be technical obsolescence. That was the fate of the life-preserver equipment materials, balsa wood and duck feathers that had been critically scarce during World War II. By the mid-1950s they had to be disposed of at a time when there was practically no demand for them. The same thing happened to quartz crystals with the development of synthetic substitutes for use in electronic equipment.

Then there are technical errors which make for costly mistakes. Again it seemed research had made an old stand-by out-of-date. For example, there was a synthetic product, atabrine, not only

---

*L. St. Clare Grondona, *Vitalizing World Abundance*, George Allen and Unwin (London, 1958). See also United Nations Conference on Trade and Development, 'The Case for An International Commodity Reserve Currency', contributed paper No. 7 by A. G. Hart, Nicholas Kaldor and Jan Tinbergen (Geneva, 1964).

as good as natural quinine, but cheaper too. However, when troops came down with fever in South Vietnam, the new synthetic did not work. Fortunately, the United States had sold off a part, but not all, of its stockpile of quinine.

Both technological obsolescence and errors in technical judgement can be anticipated. Since ours is a high-technology society it requires special emphasis on the need for both preserving options and hedging. It also means that one cannot be rigid about stockpile plans. Technological uncertainty makes it impossible to plan accurately what the costs of a stockpile will be. However, reasonable estimates can be made for each of the alternatives and can be used to illuminate the questions confronting the decision-makers.

Such cost-and-benefit analyses will be essential in the evaluation of every technological proposal. It will also be essential to the determination of what form and condition of specific material should be selected for stocking. The systems approach will also be involved in and complicated by policy questions on international relations and stockpile management methods.

International Relations

World developments that no one planned or anticipated have made relationships between countries take on a new meaning in recent years. We live in a new way because airplanes, communication satellites, exchange rates, pipelines and ships bind us all together. Scarcity brings this interdependence forcibly to our attention whether the shortage is in food, minerals, oil or timber. At such times we awaken to the reality that all of us, wherever we are, are living on the same reserves of natural resources.

When a few great industrial powers dominated the world, force (usually military, occasionally economic) assured the commercial, financial and industrial greats that their requirements were met. Political power was for a long time chiefly a function of military superiority. With the acceptance of the 'total war' concept the political-military power became a function of economic strength. When science emerged as a tool for military and industrial use, the political-military-economic relationship was measured in terms of a country's technological achievement.

At first glance, this would seem to put control in the hands of the super-powers. For a long time it did. Producers of raw materials and their customers were tied together by complementary interests which on balance favored the buyer. The customer usually could shop among a number of possible suppliers and make the decisions on who, how much and at what price.

The enormous increase in consumption of raw materials in recent years both in absolute terms and also relative to currently available supplies changed all that. Oil dramatizes the nature of the change. Now the sellers determine who will get their product, at what time, in what quantity, and at what price. Many new countries are involved, sixty-five new nations since 1960. And, the use of force has become unpopular and unlikely. Political, commercial and military alliances like the United Nations, Common Market, Warsaw Pact and NATO as well as indigenous natural resources have given new rights and new clout to those formerly less powerful.

Since World War II, gunboat diplomacy has become impractical. One result of this change has been to make the advanced industrial states more vulnerable to threats and actions by small powers that happen to be sitting on a pile of essential raw materials. The small sheikdoms of the Middle East issued their imperialistic challenges in 1973. Since the advanced industrial states had come to take oil imports for granted (developing countries did too) the result was an economic earthquake felt throughout the world.

Suddenly, the co-ordinates of international politics had shifted. The changed conditions imposed a new dimension on relationships between countries requiring additional supplies of raw materials and those controlling exportable surplus. The power in the equation for relationships between the 'imperialist greats' and their poor cousins had been reversed.

One indicator of the new situation was the action program put forth by the developing countries at the United Nations Special Session on Raw Materials and Development in April 1974. The proposal called for greater rights in sovereignty over natural resources without reference to existing international law or rights of compensation. It also asked for more commodity agreements, more producer cartels, more processing in producing countries, and no new investment in research and development for substitutes. Although most industrial countries expressed reservations, it was adopted without a vote.

This was a declaration and demonstration that the smaller nations who had materials within their borders had come of age. Pawns could now aspire to the role of bishop, even queen, now that non-renewable resources had become king.

The depression and its cut in demand has taken some of the wind out of the sails of the material cartel ships. However, unless something happens to again suddenly reverse the co-ordinates of international power, this will be only a delay and not a change in direction or plan of action. This is the atmosphere in which we must work out our policy for acceptable supply conditions.

Economic Growth Rates

National policy on the use of natural resources in all countries has been a heritage from the era of carefree abundance. It calls for economic growth based on lavish use of the difficult-to-replace bounty of nature. If we are to avoid an economic breakdown, we must face disagreeable facts, abandon old habits and make difficult choices to develop national policy appropriate for a world in which natural resources are scarce and expensive rather than abundant and cheap as they used to be.

In the simplest terms, we will have to re-examine that generally accepted national objective – economic growth. In the United States between 1900 and 1970:

A. Population climbed from 76 million to over 200 million people.
B. Gross national product expanded from around $100 billions to about $1 trillion (in 1967 dollars).
C. Natural Resource consumption (excluding food) increased from $7 to $35 billions.
D. Energy utilization went from $2 billions to more than $20 billions a year.

The 1970–3 data show even faster rates of growth which fostered demands that resulted in crisis situations in a number of basic materials (energy being only one of them).

An oversimplified outline of the modern economy can be put in these terms. Individuals wish to acquire goods. Producers increase output to meet the demand. This means more jobs and probably greater earnings for every worker. The newly employed together with the employees who are earning more, have additional money to spend or save. In either case, more production is called for, the economy grows and more non-renewable resources are used.

As indicated above, growth of GNP in the United States at a rate of four to five times that of population has required an increase in materials consumption equal to the expansion in national production, and for energy the expansion has been the double of that, about tenfold. The inter-relationship among population, GNP, materials and energy must be kept in mind in the formulation of policies for national economic growth for the future. Realism dictates that such policies distinguish between the period for which change is very difficult or impossible,

1976–85, and the years for which improvements can be effected if we act quickly, that is, the post-1985 years.

Although there are optimistic economic forecasts for 1976 and the succeeding years, the writer does not agree with them for a number of reasons. First they all assume:

A. Petroleum supply, price and payment problems have been successfully resolved.
B. Keynesian solutions will work again without creating runaway inflation.
C. That we know what to do and will do it quickly.

The lack of realism in these assumptions is fully demonstrated not only by the business and government behavior that we have seen since October 1973 in oil but also by what was not done in the pre-1973 years, especially from the mid-1960s on.

Even the optimists see the business downtrend extending into 1976 and a revival yielding growth rates for the next decade that are half or less than those of the late 1960s and substantially lower than the early 1970s. They describe the 1973–5 slide as one side of a V–shaped curve with a bottom at the end of 1975 or early 1976. They then have growth rates going smoothly up again.

Our analysis of the business turn and forecast are detailed in a later chapter. We see something more like a cellar. Graphically there is a sharp drop from 1973 (November) bottoming in 1976, then extending flat in real terms for several years with the revival starting at a low rate and moving slowly into the 1980s. This really cannot be changed significantly now. Major change required action in 1974 (even earlier). If we act on resource expansion in 1976, the long-range impact of the depression can be ameliorated and turned into a boon, that is if we put our money into expanding natural resource supply not just unemployment relief. Such expenditures can be non-inflationary now, can provide greater stimulus than any workable alternative and resolve the critical material supply problems for the 'good old' growth rates that can start around 1985.

There is no quick or easy way back to growth. Keynesian demand management means ruinous inflation and stagnation under present conditions. A belated but essential program for investing in energy and other natural resources expansion is the way out. It will minimize the misery impact of depression now with minimal inflation, and it will provide the essential base for future growth through continuously expanding consumer demand. That brings us around to our management proposal.

Management Method for the United States

Although we should like to go through a country-by-country analysis, I shall use again the United States as our illustration, chiefly, as before, because it is based on close personal experience, but also because the economic heartbeats of the United States affect the pulse of national economies all over the world.

As has probably been clear up to now, we believe that we are facing a crisis that is junior only to the 1930s Great Depression or World War II.

When Franklin D. Roosevelt instituted crisis management to meet the exigencies of economic depression in the 1930s, institutions quaked and politicians watched on with alarm. But strong, dramatic leadership overcame doubt and we rode through a period of creative government that confronted crisis with action.

At the time of World War II, crisis management was practically automatic. War itself dramatized the need and no salesmanship was necessary. Today, although there are no big bangs from guns and rockets, no visible enemy, the crisis is one of wartime proportions. The present threat from depression, oil problems and natural resource scarcities is one of critical proportions.

The American Government hasn't acted as though the country was in real trouble. But it is! And it's big trouble that can only be handled by crisis management similar to that of the 1930s and World War II. If we want to get back to the expanding or growing economy, we must create again an Office of Emergency Management.

Today we all agree on the existence of one pressing problem: depression. Because of it, the energy crisis seems less urgent and the early 1970s concern over 'limits to growth' has practically disappeared. The reality is that energy and other natural resources will again be short when, as and if, we get back to an economic growth rate of 4 per cent or higher per annum. Since that is probably ten years away, public policy today should undertake to minimize and turn around the depression forces by measures which will provide employment, stimulate business and direct investment into the expansion of supplies of energy and other basic materials.

We have yet to face up to any of these. That is, our anti-depression measures are inadequate. Our energy efforts are just a bit more than business-as-usual rather than crisis measures. And, although material shortages were acute even in mid-1974, we have no program for the natural resource scarcities that will enable recovery in the 1980s.

The dimensions of the depression, the energy problem and the future scarcities for most materials call for a pragmatic solution. What can we expect now when we look at what the Government did during the fiscal years of 1974 and 1975, and proposes to spend on energy in fiscal 1976? The President's budget shows:

	1973	1974	1975	1976
Energy:	$500m.	$606m.	$1,454m.	$2,240m.

It is really weird to visualize an economy of $1.3 trillion in 1973 and probably over $1.6 trillion by 1976, spending less than half of 1 per cent of its product to fight a crisis. And, when we eliminate the national security weapons and basic science in those figures, the numbers get smaller. Major energy expenditures for operating expense and plant and equipment are shown in detail in Table 2.1. The totals are ridiculously small for a crisis, and, when we take out the nuclear portion, the size of the energy expenditures is very hard to understand.

If the depression, energy, and materials problems are real, we must adopt a management method, such as the one the United States used successfully in World War II, to handle them. That means setting up a top economic agency like 1941's Office of Emergency Management. It was that Agency, located in the Executive Office of the President, which provided the base for the War Production Board, War Manpower Commission, Office of Civilian Supply and Price Administration and expanded uses of the Reconstruction Finance Corporation. Only with a co-ordinating and directing agency such as the Office of Emergency Management can meaningful analyses of a Manhattan Project for Coal, government-owned stockpiles, wage and price controls, and the other interdependent actions and authorities that are required, be brought into focus quickly.

The relations between government, business and private individuals must be on the same basis as in 1942–5, as that is the only way to get the speed and direction the current depression, materials and energy predicaments require. If American activity in determining the nature of the energy crisis, what should be done about it and how it should be done, continuing as in 1974–5 and projected for 1976, is a representative sample of its public policy, there is not much that we can expect and even less to hope for.

It is clear that a new deal in materials and energy is required. Equally clear is that a new approach to the depression is essential. Over the next five to ten years, we must invest at least $1 trillion in energy expansion and about the same amount in expanding

Table 2.1 Major Federal Energy Expenditures 1974, 1975 and 1976 in Millions of Dollars

	FY 1974 ACTUAL		FY 1975 ESTIMATED		FY 1976 ESTIMATED	
	Current	*Plant and Equipment*	*Current*	*Plant and Equipment*	*Current*	*Plant and Equipment*
Coal	62.6	—	174.2	13.2	279.5	20.0
Petroleum and Gas	7.9	0.1	17.3	—	33.6	0.1
Shale	2.8	—	3.5	0.1	8.1	0.3
Solar	3.9	—	8.8	0.1	57.1	—
Geothermal	6.2	0.2	13.8	1.0	28.4	0.6
Nuclear						
Fusion Power	53.0	4.5	85.0	20.3	120.0	24.2
Fission Power	286.3	148.6	384.1	205.6	444.7	159.5
Materials	511.4	233.2	646.1	262.4	828.9	405.7
Conservation						
Electric Power Transmission	1.5	0.1	6.4	0.3	11.8	1.7
Automobile Power Plant	1.5	—	4.5	—	8.2	—
Energy Storage	1.7	0.1	5.8	0.2	9.1	0.8
Consumer	—	—	—	—	3.0	—

Source: President's Budget Proposal for FY 1976

other natural resource supplies. Expenditures at that level probably mean outlays of around $5 billion the first year, $20–$50 billion the second, and around $100 billion a year thereafter. Private business should be used as much as possible, but to push entrenched Federal bureaucracy and minimize the delaying force of entrenched business interest, policy action must include legislation to provide:

A. An Office of Emergency Management to deal with overall Federal management of depression and natural resource problems including energy.

B. A Reconstruction Finance Corporation agency with power to borrow, buy and sell through private or public corporations. Initial capital $20 billion plus Government guaranteed borrowing up to $200 billion.

C. An undertaking similar to the Manhattan Project for energy. Initial funding of $5 billion in 'No-Year Obligation Authority' with Congressional Appropriation for additional borrowing.

D. TVA corporations for each of the major materials.

Illustrative of the way it could work, a Manhattan Project corporation for energy would create a Coal Expansion Corporation which, in turn would enter into long-term contracts for coal for electric utilities at prices fixed for the next ten years for both mining suppliers and their utility customers. If necessary, it would enter also into contracts for stripping shovels and conveyors, railroad cars and locomotives, right-of-way acquisition and preparation, labor training and movement, and infrastructure in new areas. In short, it would get on with the job now rather than talk about planning for it.

In the same way an Energy Conservation Corporation would be set up. It would subsidize installation of weather-stripping and insulation in existing structures, work with home financing organizations to provide better interest rates for units embodying conservation measures and speed-up introduction of new standards for energy saving in consumer durables, industrial and commercial equipment.

The above are just two illustrations of what is possible in a long list of actions that need to be taken now. It is hoped that they readily translate into a picture of jobs and business expansion. If they do, it should show a way out of the depression. If we try to do it through ten million automobiles a year, or two million housing units, or both, we shall be right back in the energy crisis and materials scarcity kettle again. So if we are going to get out of the pot and stay out of it, an investment program of the kind sketched here can do it.

3. Energy Scarcity and Public Policy

Not too many years ago energy meant something that young children and puppy dogs had too much of. Now, it's suddenly something we do not seem to be able to get enough of. This sudden discovery of the other side of the energy coin comes after we have spent much time and effort locking ourselves into a life-style and way of doing business that current arrangements for providing energy just cannot support.

Our present energy predicament is the legacy of many years in which the countries of the world were unwilling to undertake meaningful, long-range natural resources planning. Instead, they took it for granted that the supply of imported oil as well as other raw materials was endless. Although the change seemed to happen suddenly with the October 1973 Arab oil embargo, the new relationship has been developing for some years. The phenomenal economic growth and prosperity of the industrialized world since 1950 has been based on an ever-increasing use of energy. That prosperity has been translated into personal income to be spent for leisure time, travel, boating and other activities in which energy was consumed in substantial quantity.

When the *per capita* and total consumption curves started to show sharp rates of increase in energy use, a few voices were raised in warning of trouble just ahead. This led to studies, all of which attested to the validity of the warning.

One analysis so impressed the then head of the United States Department of the Interior, Secretary Rogers C. B. Morton, that he said, 'Someday somebody's going to walk into a Secretary of Interior's office and set a gallon of oil on the desk and say, "By the way, boss, this is the last gallon of oil. I don't know whether you should drink it or put it in a museum! But there it'll be." And when the time comes, this is going to be a rather disturbing thing.'

It is now clear that the realization of Secretary Morton's dire prediction will never come to pass. Nonetheless, although neither the United States nor the industrialized world is down to its last gallon of oil, the situation at the time of writing and for the immediate years ahead is going to be a difficult one. This is the result of our failure to:

1. Be realistic about the fact that energy demand was overtaking supply and that the rate of increase in consumption was accelerating at many times that of supply.
2. Develop and implement long-term programs to do something about the reality of this situation through:
   A. Earlier and more intensive exploration for new local sources of oil such as the North Sea and other coastal waters.
   B. Stabilizing rates of consumption by tax, stockpiling, import control and related measures.
   C. Research and development of substitutes for petroleum.
   D. Conservation of energy through legal prescription or tax encouragements.
   E. Substitute forms of transportation for the major user of oil, the automobile.
3. Adopt early measures for handling pollution problems in terms of a total resource system.
4. Recognize the long lead-time—two years to build railroad loco-motives and cars that are needed to expand coal output, five years or more for coal liquification and gasification and decades for shale oil extraction processes.

The difficulties we face are not just the current ones. The scarcity-induced problems will be with us well into the 1980s. If we immediately recognize that short-term, stop-gap measures just will not do, then we can start to balance supply and demand in new terms for the late 1980s and the balance of the century.

Time is the critical factor. Since we did little or nothing to develop alternative sources of energy in the 1960s and only talked about them in terms of environmental considerations such as thermal pollution, radiation and waste disposal for nuclear plants, erosion and attendant hazards from strip mining for coal, emission problems in steam conversion of shale sands into oil or gas, in the first half of the 1970s, the years immediately ahead will be bleak ones. This is the case regardless of the policy implemented by the members of the Council of Petroleum Exporting Countries.

Oil from the North Sea and Alaska will help with probably four to six million barrels a day by 1985. New discoveries could be an added bonus. But even if bonanzas, they cannot solve the supply problems created by rates of growth in energy demand such as those of the early 1970s.

Table 3.1 highlights the rapid growth in oil usage over the last decade.

Table 3.1

Country	Consumption in 1972 as a multiple of 1963
Total World	207
France	208
Germany, West	178
Italy	211
Japan	469
United Kingdom	200
United States	172
Africa	203
Communist Countries	207

Although the grand total only doubled, Western Europe's almost trebled, and Japan scored close to a quintuple. A good illustration of what was happening was the situation in the United States. There, *per capita* consumption by mid-1973 was increasing twice as fast as the population.

At that rate of growth in demand, there is no likely short-term solution and a long-term one must be projected beyond the turn of the twenty-first century. That means that the only way to correct the early 1970s imbalance over the next decade must be found on the demand side since we run into physical limits and time problems on the supply side. To do it means cutting down on current usage and putting new requirements at a figure as close to zero as is possible.

Cutting down on current usage means a reduction in the manufacture of additional cars, boats, air conditioners and a host of other energy users that we have long taken for granted. It also affects many other things we have come to take for granted, for example air conditioners set at 67°F and heating systems at 74°F. It means that we will once again find the winters are cold and the summers hot; and that most household tasks can be performed by human energy as well as by motor driven appliances. Some leisure-time problems will be solved by the increased hours required for the routine activities that are day-today living; and recreation will have to be found in the home, the neighborhood and the community, because of the high cost of the energy required in today's car trips, boating, fishing and the other activities that now dominate recreation.

It is clear that we must move from sharp expansion to maximum contraction. Even effective conservation and greater efficiency in existing energy conversion mean that the United States, for example, still would have a deficit position on the supply side at 1972 levels. And, this position cannot be handled by money. Even with petroleum imports restored at the old or slightly higher levels, population growth precludes increases in *per capita* consumption at the 1970–3 rates.

Then comes the truly bitter pill of cutting back energy demand. That is the economic situation when we have sharply curtailed production of automobiles, air conditioners, motor boats and a long list of other energy consumers. Zero or negative growth in the national economy: we should know what that means from current personal experience. We would like to believe that the miles of words that have already addressed the 'crisis' had resolved it by the time this book is in print. Surely, shortly thereafter.

Unfortunately, we cannot find that pot of gold. More discouraging, we do not even see the rainbow that might follow at the end of the present energy storm. Thus, it is appropriate that the exercise on public policy questions in natural resources be applied to energy.

Public Policy for Energy

Although there are significant differences among countries based on past, present and probable future requirements and availability of energy, all the major issues can be identified to the problem in the United States. To be sure, variations from that norm will be substantial but it is nonetheless appropriate for all in terms of policy.

As we see them, the issues are:

1. *Degree of United States dependence on foreign supplies*
    A. Quantitative terms
    B. Geographic origin
    C. Stockpiling
    D. International relations

2. *Approach to expansion of United States domestic supplies*
    A. Nuclear
            i. Breeder reactor

   ii. Other generators

   iii. Environment, security and other considerations

 B. Non-nuclear

   i. Conservation

    Industry

    Commercial and residential

    Transportation

   ii. Substitution

    Coal for oil and gas

     Developing additional supplies

     Environmental issues

     Labor supply problems

   iii. Solar

   iv. Geothermal

   v. Oil and gas

    Petroleum

    Natural gas

    Shale

    Other

   vi. Organic sources

    Cereals

    Timber

    Other

3. *Rate of developing United States supply*

 A. Time scale

   i. Present to 1985

   ii. 1985 to 1995

   iii. Later dates

 B. Resource allocations

   i. Estimates of anticipated benefits from various scales of investment

    Calculation of feasibility of various rates of resource input

4. *Management methods*

 A. Private enterprise

   i. Without government funds

   ii. With government assistance through

    Loans

    Grants

    Subsidies

    Price guarantees

    Tariffs and quotas

 B. Government operations

   i. Research only

    ii. TVA type
    iii. Manhattan Project type

5. *Economic growth*
  A. Physical constraint–energy available
    i. Allocating limiting resource
      Part for existing stock of energy users
      Portion for new, additional users
      Percent for investment in new supply
    ii. Trade-offs in terms of alternative contributions to
      GNP
      Food
        Fertilizer
        Farm operations
      Petrochemical products
        Fibers
        Structural materials
        Other
      Various industries
      Various commercial activities
      Transportation
      Goods
      Persons
        Employment related
        Household related (school; shopping)
        Travel and recreation

The rest of this chapter will discuss major forces bearing on these public policy issues.

Energy Self-sufficiency

Several questions are involved when we talk about the United States becoming independent of imports of petroleum. The first of these is when? The second is, at what cost in terms of dollars as measures of resources? Another one is by what approach; shall it be coal, shale, geothermal, methane or nuclear, and what kind of mix of the available alternatives? There obviously are or will be some other problems. However, the final question raised by self-sufficiency always is, what relationships shall we try to maintain with existing and potential foreign suppliers of energy products?

The fundamental problem is time. Just as ex-President Nixon had to revise the original goal of Project Independence from 'capacity for self-sufficiency by 1980' to the more appropriate 'capability of becoming self-sufficient in the foreseeable future', so the United States must recognize the fact that it will require oil imports for quite a few years—at least until 1985, maybe 1995—probably forever. So, unless America is willing to undergo a measure of discomfort and economic dislocation substantially greater than anyone has talked about yet, then she had better stay on good terms with her Indonesian, African, South American, Canadian and Middle-East suppliers.

The problem of time will have to be managed even before we decide on which approach to select and the degree of self-sufficiency to be sought for the late 1980s or thereafter. Freedom from dependence on foreign sources means costs both in terms of resources to be used and a new and higher price for a British Thermal Unit of energy, domestic or imported.

The level of that price and the changes and dislocations involved have had an earthquake-like impact on the country's economy and life style, which will continue not only during the period when the gap in requirements is being filled by high-priced imports, but also later on when substitutes and new supplies made possible by much higher prices are in use.

All of us now know something about the discomfort, disruption and depression that has resulted from the recent OPEC policies on supply and price for petroleum imports. To free the United States from the threat of a re-run of that drama, the National Academy of Engineers calculated that the investment required would mean direct costs of $600 billion in 1973 dollars. Adding only financial charges and an inflation factor makes the ten-year bill a trillion or so.*

But that is only the investment necessary to replace imports with domestic production. It does not take account of trade with Venezuela, for example. It does not include relationships with Canada and other cultural and trading partners. Changes of this kind defy dollar accounting terms and yet they are among the major costs to be borne by a United States policy of self-sufficiency in energy.

Net Energy

At the same time that the United States decides to invest billions of dollars in an effort to make the country self-sufficient in energy,

---

*Although this is a discussion of United States requirements, it is interesting to note that the OECD report 'Long-Term Energy Assessment' estimates an investment requirement of $1.1 trillion in 1972 dollars for development of domestic energy resources to their 'full potential for the group'. The OECD group of experts was headed by Professor Hans K. Schneider, Director, Institute for Energy Economics, University of Cologne. The Institute's work was well under way before the energy situation reached crisis proportions after the Yom Kippur War.

it would be wise for her to make calculations for the long term that show the energy required to produce the energy sought in its new ventures. To date, the measurement that has been applied has been dollars required with little or no recognition of the difference between the government fiat that is responsible for paper money, and the non-replaceable fossil fuel and other scarce natural resources involved in the proposals for new domestic supplies of energy.

When a statement is made such as 'we have an 800-year supply of coal in this country', no provision is made for the energy required to open up the new mining areas, operate the mines and at the end of the operation to return the land to useable condition. In the case of strip mining, coal can be extracted but only after tons and tons of overburden have been pushed aside. Then when the pit is worked out, the earth must be bull-dozed back into the hole and the entire area contoured, covered with topsoil, seeded and processed for a long period of time.

The Environment Policy Center's Joseph Browder claims that the energy cost of stripping coal in the American Northern Great Plains also should include the loss of energy involved when live-stock now produced on the native grasses must be replaced by livestock produced in a feed lot that depends on energy–intensive fertilizers and irrigation. These costs in producing the displaced protein, he contends, must be added to the others just described.*

If we intend to liquify or gasify the coal, there probably will be a need to develop additional water sources–again, this involves substantial costs in energy. According to the President's Council on Environmental Quality, physical losses of energy in strip-mined coal through processing and transportation, or in electric power conversion through heat losses in power plants, and leakage on transmission lines, now amount to around 70 per cent. In real terms, only 30 per cent of the energy now reaches the final user.

If we add on the energy consumed in the capital outlays for preparing for mining, reclamation, alternative protein supplies,

---

*Although not directly related to the development of coal production in the Northern Great Plains, the relationship between energy and food production may be of interest to some readers, and they are referred to '*US Agriculture is Growing Trouble as Well as Crops*', by Wilson Clark, *Smithsonian*, January 1975, p. 59. A few quotations as well as the title pretty much tell the story:

'The production of fertilizers and farm chemicals require extensive use of fossil fuel energy.'

'Another high energy user in modern mechanized agriculture is irrigation.'

'Powering the more than five million tractors in the US (on farms) requires eight billion gallons of fuel per year.'

'It takes as much energy to run the tractors as is contained in the food produced. Some experts wonder how long we can keep this up.'

additional water and the like, the net energy yield shrinks even more. This could reduce an 800-year supply of coal by one-half or three-quarters.

What has been happening in the nuclear field underscores the need for including in the supply estimates, the energy required to produce the additional energy. According to Professor E. J. Hoffman, a nuclear specialist at the University of Wyoming: 'As much as half of the gross electrical output of a nuclear plant would have to be recycled to supply input for fuel processing.' When uranium exploration, mining, refining and transporting, plus waste disposal and other energy demands are added on, Dr. Hoffman concludes: 'The cumulative energy expenditure of the entire atomic energy program may not be recouped from the nuclear fission power plants by the time the reserve of economically recoverable U-235 is used up.'

Dr. Hoffman's concept of the net energy yield from nuclear power as well as the data on the final energy derived from strip-mined coal developed by the President's Council on Environmental Quality are cited here only as reasons for making new calculations when we formulate energy policy. We must distinguish between energy inputs and money inputs. Dollars can no longer be used as proxies for coal, oil and gas. Instead, cost and benefit analyses must also be made in physical terms for energy resources used and net energy produced.

Management Methods

Once we have established an overall strategy for energy research, development and production, we must then determine the method by which we will manage our efforts to achieve the goal 'to attain by 1980 (or President Ford's 1985) the capability of becoming self-sufficient in the foreseeable future' (or any other designated alternate). It seems clear that government is expected to pay the research bill. From then on, the government could operate on its own, enter into partnerships with industry to ensure that the energy technology is developed into commercial application, or make the technology freely available and assume that the profit potential would attract industry into general uses of the new techniques.

There also are those who believe that all that is needed to bring about self-sufficiency is the operation of the forces of the free market. That scenario proceeds as follows: as prices rise, consumption is cut back and available supply fills the needs of those who are able to pay more. Higher prices force a better use of available energy, for example, coal, and they cite Sasol

(South African Coal, Oil and Gas Corporation) which produces oil from coal, profitably. Then they point out possibilities for product re-design, conservation and so on, which they assume would be the free market response to higher oil and energy prices.

Following much the same line of reasoning, there are those who would keep government action or 'interference' at a minimum. A good statement of this position was provided in 1974 by an independent consultant to the petroleum industry, Walter J. Levy, whose proposal can be summarized as follows: (1) put leasing for the outer continental shelf on a 'regularized and expedited' basis; (2) decontrol natural gas prices; (3) provide new tax incentives for secondary and tertiary recovery; (4) guarantee profit margins for synthetic oil and gas; (5) eliminate the kind of government activity that has interfered with the development of nuclear energy, the Alaskan pipeline and meaningful oil import programs.

This view has gained wide approval. Nonetheless, there are many demands for government action. The Administration's proposal as incorporated in the budget for the 1976 fiscal year placed the major emphasis on cutting current consumption through import duties and excise taxes that make energy more costly. It also included small programs, in dollar terms, for increasing energy efficiency of major electrical appliances, for reducing heating requirements through insulation, storm windows and weather stripping in existing housing, and for improved design for energy saving in new construction.

To expand supply, President Ford's approach concentrated on research and development. Little or no provision has been made for exploiting the new technology that this research and development may produce. Almost six months later, this position was again taken in the government's new energy development plan. On 30 June, 1975 a 'national plan for energy research, development and demonstration', ordered by Congress, was made public by the Energy Research and Development Administration.

President Ford said in releasing the report: 'We are not talking about tomorrow, we're talking about 25 years from now or more. The function performed is not necessary for us but for our children and our grandchildren.'

That was the very point made by Robert C. Seamans, Jr. head of ERDA and his associates. However, the essence of the program may be found in Mr. Seaman's statement that spending in the 1976 fiscal year would rise by nearly 20 per cent, to $57 million. Then, even he had to say, 'the total did seem small'.

The present and proposed research efforts aim chiefly at improving the production and use of coal plus harnessing the energy of the atom. This includes mining technology, coal liquification and gasification, as well as emission control techniques to permit burning coal with a high sulphur content. There is provision for continued work on the demonstration breeder reactor power station on the Clinch River in Tennessee. Smaller amounts of funding are proposed for solar and geophysical research and for conservation technology. Of a proposal to spend some $2 billion on current-action and future-oriented research in fiscal year 1976, about one-half would go to further development of nuclear energy.

The 1976 spending proposals seem grossly inadequate for the goals to be attained in the 1980s. The Federal Energy Administration's Project Independence Report provided an optimistic comparison for what it expected from an 'Accelerated Development Program' compared to 'Business as Usual' as shown in Table 3.2. It is hoped all the figures in the accelerated development program are the hard data for 1985 and not just another set of hopeful guesstimates. The smallness of the gain shown for nuclear production probably reflects the result of recent discouraging events overtaking earlier optimism. Unfortunately, that may also be the fate of the presently optimistic figures for coal gasification, shale oil and some other hoped-for 'solutions' to the problem.

Table 3.2   Estimated 1985 Production Potential based on $11 per Barrel of Oil

Energy Form	Business as Usual	Accelerated Development
Oil	15 million barrels a day	20 million
Natural Gas	23 trillion cubic feet/year	29 trillion
Coal	1.1 billion tons/year	2.1 billion
Coal gasification	0.1 trillion cubic feet/year	1.0 trillion
Coal liquification	——	500,000 barrels/day
Shale oil	250,000 barrels/day	1.0 million
Nuclear	234 million kilowatts	275 million
Geothermal	6000 megawatts	15,000
Solar electricity	41 million megawatts/year	150 million
Solar heating and cooling	0.3 quadrillion Btus	0.60 quadrillion

The dim outlook is made darker by the more than two years of confused and inadequate approaches to managing the energy situation. Because there are no big bangs from guns and rockets in 1975, we are still talking a lot and doing very little. The dimensions of the national energy problem and the depression, which is largely energy related, call for a pragmatic solution.

Although the competitive market has been a great tool for some two centuries, war and depression–National Emergency–have always forced its temporary abandonment. The view that 'working through great corporations that straddle the earth, men are able for the first time to utilize world resources with an efficiency dictated by the objective logic of profit', has great appeal. The words are those of a partner in the international investment-banking firm of Lehman Brothers, who served as an Under-Secretary of State under Presidents Kennedy and Johnson.

But both prior to 1973 and since, the global giants have failed to put the appropriate plans into effect. They have not acted on their own account nor have they proposed and lobbied for meaningful public policy. We cannot afford to be slaves to the tradition that the least government is the best government when our economic system has produced actual and potential social losses beyond the capacity of the market to absorb. The government must act quickly, cover all possible lines of action and employ resources as though it was waging a war. It is too late now to talk about what should have been done.

Our illustration of the Management Method for United States Policy in Chapter 2, based on an energy example, makes it clear that a New Deal in energy is required. Given the present managers and their apparent satisfaction with their methods, only public debate along the lines we propose can provide real promise for the United States.

'No-policy' Energy Policy

United States energy policy has always developed in bits and pieces from a variety of power centers. Until late in 1973, the power centers were The Oil Policy Committee, five of the executive departments–Commerce, Defense, Interior, State and Treasury, and a long list of regulatory and administrative agencies, e.g., Federal Power Commission and Environmental Protection Agency. By seemingly deliberate design as much as by accident, not one of these offices saw the total energy problem, and each one seemed to consider and represent only a small part of all of the interests involved.

Ideally, creating the Federal Energy Office and its successor the Federal Energy Administration would have provided the vehicle for a comprehensive and effective energy policy. In reality, because those who had had the most influence in the past managed to hang on to their traditional roles, the new agency neither eliminated the previous problems in bringing together a 'co-ordinated' policy nor established itself as the final authority on policy.

Congress, its committees, presidential aides, Office of Management and Budget, courts, state and local government, big business, small business and individuals each see and react to proposals for energy policy as it affects them. This makes formulation, enactment and enforcement of an energy program difficult, but not impossible. Obviously, if we do not have a specific policy, the absence of one constitutes the national policy. Nonetheless, since we are convinced that the situation will continue as it has been – no meaningful policy proposals by the President, Congress or anyone else – we will review the post-embargo developments and then offer our own proposal for what we consider essential policy.

The record starts in 1973 when the then American President, Mr. Nixon announced a new policy that was to make the country independent of foreign supplies of petroleum by 1980. Early in 1974, this was restated more realistically as 'capability of becoming self-sufficient in the foreseeable future'. At the end of that year, the Federal Energy Administration published a *Project Independence Report*. The substance of its meaning was summarized in the tabulation of potential 1985 energy supplies in Table 3.2.

President Ford subsequently augmented Project Independence Policy. He aimed at cutting back imports by a million barrels a day and increasing domestic production. A tariff on imported crude, elimination of domestic oil price ceilings, excise taxes and regulatory measures were implementing actions. It was pointed out by Congressmen, economists and the press that this would lead to higher prices, not only for all energy, but also for all goods. It drew opposition from many sides.

The Democratic Congress then came up with a proposal to cut back consumption through conservation that would take effect only over a period of quite a few years. The Democrats were prepared to do great things in the 1980s. However, they seemed reluctant to impose any immediate and significant change in the ways that Americans lived, drove and consumed energy in the intervening years. Their policy offered little promise of cutting America's oil imports in the current years except by quota limits on imports. It meant continuing the country's dependence on foreign oil until well into the 1980s.

It was not at all clear that the Executive's position was all that different when in March 1975, two officials of the Federal Energy Administration told the Congress:*

> There is no longer a general shortage of crude oil or petroleum products, with the possible exception of propane . . . Crude oil is freely available . . . World-wide refinery capacity has increased . . . Stock levels are near record highs . . . In short, in many ways, the market has returned to near the normal conditions that prevailed in 1972.

From this came the inevitable newspaper headline 'Energy Officials say, Crisis is Over.'

And all of this without referring to the new price level and its impact on world-wide consumption, the depression, the mild winters of 1974–5 and 1973–4. Most important, it completely neglected increased entries of foreign oil.

If the United States is not prepared to reduce its petroleum imports sharply–not in the 1980s but right now–it must recognize that it becomes even more dependent than before on the Persian Gulf producers. For a variety of reasons, traditional major suppliers, Canada and Venezuela, have been reducing their shipments to the United States and other outsiders have been increasing their share of the market.

Let's start with the reality that about 40 per cent of the United States supply of crude oil and refined products in 1975 was imported, and the proportion of Middle Eastern oil was not declining. That means that the United States was even more vulnerable to Arab generated changes in supply and price terms than in 1973. Although there had been a great deal of talk about buffer stocks (national and international) and joint assistance and action, meaningful results are not yet in sight.

Although consumption has declined because of the combined impact of mild winters, the four-fold price increase, and the depression, we have in no sense reduced United States dependence on imported oil. Conservation had a brief vogue in late 1973 and the first quarter of 1974. Since then it has been 'light up the skies' once again. As one wit has put it, 'what can you expect of a nation that never has been able to teach its children to turn out the lights on leaving the room or its adults to drive slow.' Even though the present need for conservation is not a laughing matter, no one is willing to force conservation by regula-

---

*R. E. Montgomery Jr. Counsel and G. C. Smith, Assistant Administrator, Federal Energy Administration in joint testimony submitted to a House of Representatives, Commerce Sub-Committee, March 12, 1975.

tion or taxation (the 55 mile speed limit is the noteworthy exception, although observance has waned).

Since we are not doing anything to reduce reliance on imports through conservation, it might seem fortunate that the United States (and the European Economic Community) seem to be establishing a better basis for communicating with the Arab world. If this eased the political tension, it could be added to the business depression as yet another excuse for doing nothing. As this 'no-policy' policy goes into effect, the industrialized nations of the world will continuously stand at the edge of an oil-shortage abyss. There, they will always be at the mercy of the Arabs who can push them over the edge at any time. We believe it is important to get out of that dangerous position. A successful get-away will require speed and daring.

Our Policy Proposal

We start with the proposition that the 1970–3 year-to-year rate of increase in energy consumption in the United States must be held in check until we have much, much more energy capability. Even without an Arab embargo, in mid-1973, we had outrun existing electric generating and domestic oil refining capacities. On top of that were the inadequate supplies of low-sulphur coal and oil. So, we would have had brown-outs, black-outs, queues at the gasoline pumps and price run-ups (in the absence of government price control) in any case. It is obvious that we must expand production substantially and until that is accomplished, consumption must be cut back by means other than a depression.

The other major proposition is that the threat of supply-stoppage and price-gouging must be minimized by short-run stockpiling and long-run expansion of production both in the United States and world-wide. So, whether we want to reduce oil imports to redress the balance-of-payments or want to divert a part of both imports and domestic production into a stockpile, American or international, we must cut *per capita* and total consumption below both the 1972 and the present levels.

If the United States wants to reduce dependence on the use of oil as a political weapon to be used against it, she must go far beyond anything yet done by either government or industry in the name of Project Independence. Mild winters and a depressed economy can and will create temporary gluts of petroleum products. But the United States program must be one that can handle prolonged periods of severe cold for several years in a row and also provide the energy for at least a 4 per cent rate of growth in the economy in the 1980s.

Starting with the illustration of Management Method used in Chapter 2, here in outline form for energy are the steps to be taken by the United States as we see them:

1. Recognize that although there is no visible enemy, no bombs or rockets, the current and future problem is one of war-time emergency size. This country has not yet spent or proposed to spend as much as one-half of one per cent of Gross National Product on additional investment to deal with the energy crisis.
2. Over the next ten years, we must invest at least $1 trillion in energy expansion through public and private activities.*
3. Set up an agency like 1940's Office of Emergency Management to act as that organization did before Pearl Harbor and through V-E and V-J days. It was OEM located in the Executive Office of the President that provided the base for the War Production Board, War Manpower Commission, Office of Price Administration and expanded use of the Reconstruction Finance Corporation.

   Only through a top directing and co-ordinating agency can meaningful analyses of a Manhattan Project-type undertaking for coal, government-owned stockpiles, wage and price controls and the other required interdependent actions and authorities that are essential, be brought into focus quickly.
4. Private business should be used in so far as possible. However, to minimize the delaying impact of established business interests and to push entrenched Federal bureaucracy, several new government authorities must be created as was done for World War II.
5. Legislate an institution along the lines of the Reconstruction Finance Corporation to channel funds to private and public energy expansion activities. Initial capital appropriation should be at least $20 billion with appropriation authority to borrow up to $200 billion. Over the ten-year period, the new energy RFC would put repayments into a revolving fund. It would support:
   A. Coal Expansion Authority set up in the pattern of the Manhattan Project for the Atomic Bomb. CEA would be financed by the Energy RFC and would have the power to:
      i. Finance expansion of capacity in:

---

*See footnote on page 39, also.

       a. Coal mines both old and new

       b. Essential equipment like stripping shovels, large capacity conveyors, railroad locomotives and cars, huge trucks and related vehicles.

  ii. Buy, sell and lease equipment and land for:

       a. Mines–new and old

       b. Right-of-way for new or additional rail, highway or canal transportation

       c. Additional water supplies.

 iii. Recruit and train new mining and mining-related employees. Provide:

       a. Recruiting facilities and staff

       b. Training facilities and staff

       c. Bargaining with existing employee and employer organizations on requirements, rights of new workers, wages and hours.

  iv. Buy, finance and otherwise provide new or added infrastructure requirements like:

       a. Housing

       b. Schools

       c. Hospitals

       d. Highways, roads, streets and sewers

       e. Banks

       f. Recreation facilities

   v. Buy coal or coal equivalents on long-term contracts at fixed prices.

  vi. Sell coal or coal equivalents on long-term fixed price contracts. For example, to electric utilities.

B. Energy Conservation Authority is created. It is financed by the Energy RFC. It has the power to:

   i. Develop programs for energy savings through changes in present practices, more general application of existing knowledge and accelerate introduction of new technology.

       a. Provide appropriate stimuli through proposals for regulatory and tax legislation discouraging or prohibiting bad energy use practices.

       b. Foster, develop and finance consumer education programs for various categories of users

         Household

         Industrial

         Agricultural

         Commercial

         Governmental

ii. Subsidize energy conservation in existing structures through weatherstripping, storm windows and insulation.
iii. Subsidize interest rates for new structures embodying approved conservation building materials, equipment and practices.
iv. Speed-up introduction of energy saving standards in consumer durables, industrial and commercial equipment through:
    a. Tax incentives
    b. Fixed price purchase guarantees
    c. Research, development, test and evaluation grants to laboratories in universities, governments and business.

Summing Up

This discussion has pointed out some of the major policy issues to be worked out as we formulate the United States energy program and national economic policy for the years immediately ahead and on into the twenty-first century. As indicated earlier, although there are significant differences in past, present and future requirements for energy as well as availability of energy supplies most, if not all, of each country's policy issues and management needs can be identified with those in the American situation. In the same way, all of the countries of the world must remember that resolving the energy problem rather than being a cure-all will instead open a Pandora's Box of other natural resource scarcities. If we want to avoid a series of repeats of the 1973–4 energy crisis in numerous other natural resources, we must do national planning for these scarcities now and start implementing policy for the future as soon as 1977 or 1978.

Although 1973–4 Energy Crisis, OPEC and Arab Gulf oil have all been mentioned, it should be obvious that we do not consider this as a place for one more discussion of the balance-of-payments, Arab investment or other situations produced by the oil exporters' action on price. We are concerned with a world of scarcity in terms of public policy issues presented by natural resource availability and use. In that context, the Organization of Petroleum Exporting Countries means cartel and the possibility of that kind of combined action in other natural resources.

4. Cartels

Everyone now knows what OPEC stands for: high cost of living, no jobs, inflation and many of the other undesirable features of day-to-day living since late 1973. It also stands for Organization of Petroleum Exporting Countries. This is a cartel, which is a group of producers who get together to reduce or eliminate competition in a given area of business activity. Its goal is higher profits for its participants made possible by higher prices or price maintenance and avoidance of price cutting.

For a long time, cartel meant private business agreements in contrast with inter-governmental commodity agreements. That distinction was always an academic one since cartel arrangements frequently involved some kind of government participation and were not all that different from government-sponsored commodity control schemes such as the Stevenson Plan for rubber in the early 1920s.*

Since OPEC with its controlling group, the brothers-in-blood fraternity OAPEC, The Organization of Arab Petroleum Exporting Countries, is a most successful cartel, their new method of doing business must figure prominently in any discussion of natural resource scarcities. The oil exporters' success in escalating prices and immensely boosting their own balance-of-payments surpluses has focused world attention on their cartel and possible changes in future relationships between consumers and producers of other basic materials. Making a four-fold price increase stick, looks like an extremely good deal to the producers of other basic commodities.

As a result, many raw-material exporting countries are already imitating OPEC or seriously considering how they, too, might pull it off. Price fixing, particularly higher prices, seems attractive

---

*See David Novick, 'Production Through Restriction of Output – AAA and The Stevenson Plan', *New York World Telegram* and other newspapers, 24 April 1934.

for one-material, one-crop export-oriented countries whose earnings tend to be cyclically or chronically depressed.

But it is not easy to organize a cartel and it is even harder to make it work. In the past, concerted efforts by major producers to raise commodity prices to unrealistic levels have not succeeded over any long period of time.

It is not at all clear when a cartel is a commodity agreement or vice versa. Both of them operate through export quotas, usually, but not necessarily, with controls on production and prices. This means that both restrict free choice in trade arrangements for buyers and sellers. If there really is a difference between them, it is that intergovernmental commodity agreements require consumer country representation.

What Are International Commodity Agreements?

Although there were other earlier international commodity trade arrangements prior to World War II, the Inter-American Coffee Agreement of 1940 will be singled out, because it was the first important commodity scheme in which a consuming country, the United States, not only participated in, but also arranged, the quota system on coffee exports from Latin America.

This was a variation on the earlier International Commodity Price Stabilization Agreement idea. Those pacts sought through concerted international action to mitigate the adverse effects of continuing imbalance between production and consumption, too heavy inventories and violent price swings. That approach became the basis of the provisions in the charter of the proposed International Trade Organization which was stillborn at the United Nations Havana Conference on Trade and Development in 1948. Although the proposed organization did not come into existence, the provisions of the draft charter, quoted below, set out the basis for practically all subsequent international negotiations on commodities. They were:

> . . . to prevent or moderate pronounced fluctuations in the price of a commodity with a view to achieving a reasonable degree of stability on the basis of such prices as are fair to consumers and to provide a reasonable return to producers . . . to maintain and develop the natural resources of the world and protect them from unnecessary exhaustion; to provide for the expansion of production of a primary commodity where this can be accomplished with advantage to consumers and producers . . . to assure the equitable distribution of a primary commodity in short supply.

I would like to draw attention to 'fair to consumers' as well as 'with advantage to consumers and producers'. This put the

ICA concept in a separate and different class than *producers-only cartels.*

Some of the major commodities covered by existing or earlier international agreements are wheat, sugar, tin, coffee and olive oil. These originally conformed to principles set out in the Havana Charter. That is, they were between governments and both producers and consumers were parties to the negotiations. It may be worth noting here that if OPEC were considered an International Commodity Agreement when it was put together in 1960, it went without challenge for many years for two major violations of the Havana Charter: first, the requirement for consumer representation, and second, its bargaining was not with importing *governments* but with producing and marketing *companies.*

Since the terms of trade that are now being sought by the one-commodity, one-crop countries are those of OPEC rather than inter-governmental commodity agreements, they shall be discussed in more detail.

Cartels

Effective cartels are found in concentrated marketing situations where private parties control concentrations of patents as in the chemical, glass, business machine, pharmaceutical, plastics and photography industries, or where they control access to concentrations of natural resources such as nickel in Canada and diamonds in South Africa. To that old definition we would now add the words 'governments control concentrations of'. Surely the OPEC members now control access to concentrations of the natural resource, petroleum. In the future the OAPEC may control concentrations of patents in petro-chemicals or any other industrial area.

THE ORGANIZATION OF PETROLEUM EXPORTING COUNTRIES AND THE ORGANIZATION OF ARAB PETROLEUM EXPORTING COUNTRIES

Although the above heading may seem a printing error or a play on words, it is not! First there were the annual Petroleum Congresses sponsored by the Arab League beginning in 1959. Although the formal OAPEC carries a 1968 date, it serves much the same purpose as the earlier special sessions of the Arab League. When the international oil companies cut crude prices in 1959, non-Arab Iran and Venezuela identified their interests with those of Iraq, Kuwait and Saudi Arabia and the combination formed OPEC in 1960. Later on, Indonesia, Libya, Quatar, Abu

Dhabi, Nigeria, Algeria and Ecuador joined the club. This meant that by the mid-1960s, around 75 per cent of the world's reserves, and over 90 per cent of the oil exports to non-Communist countries, were under OPEC.

OAPEC was set up as an Arab addition to OPEC by Saudi Arabia, Kuwait and Libya in 1968. Subsequently, all Arab oil exporting nations joined up. This group goes far beyond OPECs aims to raise crude oil prices, regulate production in order to stabilize prices, get a larger share of the revenues produced by oil exports, and determine prices by consultation and agreement among the governments represented in the OPEC.

There are substantive differences between the two organizations. In October 1973 the OAPEC decided to embargo oil shipments to countries that might favor Israel in the Yom Kippur War. In 1957 the Arab League created the Arab Financial Institution for Economic Development.* This has now become the Arab Capital Investment Corporation with broad business powers for joint action. There is no similar accord between the non-Arab members of OPEC.

The thirtieth anniversary advertisement of the League of Arab States on pages 56–7 provides a good summary of their aims and activities plus a list of members.

Lest we get too excited about either OAPEC or the Arabs, we shall take a quick look at the Middle East oil situation as it has developed since 1928. A new study by the United States Foreign Relations Committee, Subcommittee on Multinational Corporations, published in 1974, provides additional background on how it all came about.

At the time of World War I, the United States was the world's largest producer of petroleum, providing two-thirds of world supplies, and principal exporter. Nonetheless, there were those like President 'Teddy' Roosevelt who had already predicted that America's domestic oil resources would be exhausted in the not too distant future. This established the need for additional outside sources.

Standard Oil of New Jersey followed this line by informing the United States State Department it would like to do exploration in Iraq. State would not approve a single company venture but said it would look favorably on such an enterprise on behalf of a group of American companies. Texaco, Gulf Atlantic Refin-

---

*Although not Arab League, it is worth noting that in May 1975 Egypt, Saudi Arabia, Quatar and the United Arab Emirates formed the Arab Authority for Military Industry with $1.04 billion capital.

ing, Sinclair, and Standard of Indiana were then invited to join with Jersey (now EXXON). Anglo-Irania also decided to work with them.

The price of establishing the first American oil interest in the Middle East was the so-called Red Line Agreement of 1928. Under that pact, members agreed not to compete against one another in the old Ottoman Empire.

Partly because it was not in the Red Line Pact, and partly for other reasons, Standard Oil of California was able to buy a concession in Bahrain. In 1933 it added to this an exclusive concession in Saudi Arabia. In the process of acquiring needed capital and market outlets for the new venture, California took in a partner, Texaco. This became the foundation for the now-familiar Aramco or Arabian American Oil Company, dated 1944. By the end of World War II, the companies already identified, plus the two Shell organizations and Socony-Vacuum (Mobil), had a cartel. (Neither the first nor the last cartel in the international petroleum industry, but one essential to the Middle East oil story.)

A number of patents and a variety of marketing agreements were involved but the cartel's major control was through its basis for royalty payments. The pricing schedule was so complicated and hard to understand that it seems to have been developed more to baffle the United States Department of Justice trust busters, and lose economic analysts in a maze of twisting and turnings, than be part of a contract.

The payment procedure started with 'the posted price' which represented the dollars and cents at which the producing parts of a company sold to its refinery counterparts. A percentage of the posted price was collected in royalties by the country granting the concession. A royalty plus actual production costs (twelve cents a barrel for Saudi Arabia) were subtracted from the posted price to determine the concessionaire's profit. An income tax was then levied on the profit by the host government. For example, in the 1950s the Saudi Arabians posted price was $2.00 per barrel and the royalty was 25 cents. Income tax was 50 per cent making a total of $1.05 a barrel for the royal families.

Although the cartel cut the posted price in 1959 and in other ways seemed to dominate the picture, it had reckoned without emerging new forces like Colonel Muammar al-Quadafi in Libya. He threw out his king in September 1969. He then won a majority victory in his dealings with the oil companies (September 1970). The income tax was upped from 50 per cent to 54 per cent and the posted price increased by 30 cents. Within

30TH ANNIVERSARY ADVERTISEMENT

ORGANIZATION

THE COUNCIL
is the supreme organ of the League of Arab States, consisting of representatives of the twenty member states and Palestine.

THE SECRETARIAT
is responsible for the day-to-day administration of the Arab League, under its Sectrary-General, Mr. Mahmoud Riad, former Foreign Minister of the Arab Republic of Egypt. The Secretariat has departments of economic, political, legal, cultural, social and labor affairs, and for petroleum, finance, Palestine, health, information, communications and protocol.

THE ECONOMIC COUNCIL
was established in 1950, composed of the Ministers of Economic Affairs or their representatives.

THE COUNCIL OF ARAB ECONOMIC UNITY
was established in 1964 by the Economic Council. Its aims include removal of internal tariffs, establishing common external tariffs, freedom of movement of labor and capital, and the adoption of common economic policies.

Specialized agencies and bureaus of the Arab League include:

THE ARAB EDUCATIONAL CULTURAL AND SCIENTIFIC ORGANIZATION
established in 1964 to promote the ideas of Arab Cultural Unity and to which each member state submits an annual report on progress in education, cultural matters and science.

THE ARAB STATES BROADCASTING UNION
created in 1969 to coordinate and study broadcasting subjects, and to exchange expertise and technical cooperation. Members include 20 Arab radio and TV stations and for foreign associates.

THE ARAB LABOR ORGANIZATION
established in 1965 for cooperation in labor problems, unification of labor legislation and conditions of work, social insurance, etc.

THE CIVIL AVIATION COUNCIL OF ARAB STATES
founded in 1967 to develop the principles, techniques and economics of air trans-

port between the member states.

THE ARAB CITIES ORGANIZATION
founded in 1967 to deal with scientific, cultural and social aspects of town development, planning and administration. Membership is open to main Arab town councils.

THE JOINT DEFENSE COUNCIL
established in 1950 to implement joint defence, and consists of the Foreign Minister and Defense. Ministers or their representatives.

THE INTERNATIONAL ORGANIZATION FOR SOCIAL DEFENSE
comprises three bureaus responsible for narcotics, crime prevention, and the Bureau of Criminal Police. The Arab League maintains information offices in New York (with branches in Washington, Chicago, San Francisco and Dallas), Geneva, Bonn, Rio de Janeiro, London, New Delhi, Rome, Ottawa, Buenos Aires, Tokyo, Paris, Dakar and Nairobi. Offices are planned for Addis Ababa, Ankara, Lagos, Copenhagen and Madrid.

The League of Arab States

ALGERIA, BAHRAIN, EGYPT, IRAQ, JORDAN, KUWAIT, LEBANON, LIBYA, MAURITANIA, MOROCCO, OMAN, PEOPLE'S YEMEN, QATAR, SAUDI ARABIA, SOMALIA, SUDAN, SYRIA, TUNISIA, UNITED ARAB EMIRATES, YEMEN ARAB REPUBLIC.

THIRTY YEARS PROGRESS

1945 Pact of the Arab League signed.
1946 Cultural Treaty signed.
1950 Joint Defence and Economic Cooperation Treaty.
1953 Creation of Arab Telecommunications and Radio Communications Union. Founding of Institute of Advanced Arab Studies. Cairo First Conference of Arab Education Ministers.
1954 Formation of Arab Postal Union. Nationality Agreement.
1956 Agreement on a Common Tariff Nomenclature.
1957 Agreement on creation of Arab Financial Institution for Economic Development Cultural Agreement with UNESCO.
1958 Cooperation Agreement between Arab League and the International Labor Organization.
1959 First Arab Oil Congress.
1960 Inauguration of new Arab League HQ Midan Al Tahrir, Cairo.
1961 Agreement to establish Arab Organization for Administrative Sciences. Agreement with WHO on exchange of medical information.

1962 Agreement to establish economic unity.
1963 Agreement to establish Arab Navigation Company. Agreement to establish Arab Organization on Social Defense Against Crime.
1964 First session of the Council of Arab Information Ministers.
1965 Arab Common Market· established. Casablanca Conference of Arab Leaders, September. Establishment of Arab Air Carriers Organization. Agreement on Arab Cooperation for Peaceful Uses of Atomic Energy.
1966 Cairo Conference of Arab Leaders, March. Cairo Conference of Arab Leaders, June.
1967 Cairo Conference of Arab Foreign Ministers. Cairo Meeting of Arab Heads of State. Conference of Arab leaders, Khartoum. Establishment of Civil Aviation Council for Arab States. Agreement to establish Arab Tourist Company.
1968 First Conference of Arab Tourist Ministers. Establishment of Arab

Fund for Economic and Social Development.
1969 Summit Meeting held in Rabat. Establishment of Industrial Development Center for Arab States. First Conference of Arab Health Ministers.
1970 Establishment of Arab Organization for Agricultural Development. Establishment of Arab Educational, Cultural and Scientific Organization.
1972 Mahmoud Riad succeeds Abdel Khalck Hassouna as Secretary-General of the Arab League. First Arab Traffic Conference.
1973 Treaty for Technical Cooperation between the Afro-Asian Rural reconstruction Organization (AARRO) and Arab League signed. Declaration issued defining Arab demands for Settlement of the Middle East Conflict. Algiers Arab Summit.
1974 Agreement to establish a permanent Joint Commission for Economic Cooperation with EEC.

a few months, similar terms were used by all of OPEC. On January 1, 1975 the posted price was doubled and the income tax rate set at 55 per cent.

In addition to increasing their revenues through those actions, several of the countries followed Libya in nationalizing foreign oil company holdings on their territory. This trend reached a temporary stop in an October 1972 agreement that stated that producing countries would buy 25 per cent of their oil tenants at the outset and increase their holdings to 51 per cent by 1982.

All of this was made possible by the sudden jump in oil consumption in the industrialized countries, particularly in Japan and Europe at the end of the 1960s. In 1970 the annual report prepared by OPEC noted:

> The year under review . . . marks a turning point . . . which seems to have put an end to a long era of cheap oil and a buyers' market and to have ushered in an era of firm prices and a sellers' market for oil.

That continued to be the climate for several more years, both before and after the Yom Kippur War. Now that production has had to be cut back substantially and may have to be further reduced to maintain the price, the cartel may have to learn a new formula for its continuing existence and success. As of mid-1975, the cartel seems to have grown increasingly adroit in managing its affairs.

The OPEC brings together countries in three entirely different economic situations. First there are the ones like Gabon, Qatar, Kuwait, Libya, the Emirates and Saudi Arabia which for a long time, cannot put their revenues into socially productive uses. Then there are the countries which desperately need every penny they can get right now, for example, Ecuador, Indonesia and Nigeria. The third group is typified by Iran and Venezuela which have dedicated their oil income to economic and social development of their countries.

The last category is interested in quick, big returns, so they want the highest price they can get for the largest quantity they can sell. That means they will cut production a little if the total return remains higher but total dollars are their goal. Those in difficult financial straits, such as Indonesia, Ecuador and Nigeria want high prices and will only forego production if someone donates to them the money they give up by 'no sale' action. So it is up to Saudi Arabia to keep them happy, that is pay them off, if they want to keep the cartel ship from springing a price-cut leak.

To return to cartels in general, however structured, they fix prices, restrict and direct shipments, and divide markets and major outlets to obtain profits that are greater than those which would be realized in a competitive market. This may lead to pooling arrangements so that members who withhold goods do not incur losses for their co-operation with those who have been able to deliver at the artificially higher price.

The basic purpose is to create and support prices that are higher than they otherwise would be. Price fixing with control of production, stocks and shipments is the method usually used. By setting prices that are above the ones needed to cover the costs of even the least efficient producer, all members of the cartel obtain more in profits than they could get in competition with one another.

Since the artificially high price invites competition which would drive down the price, the successful cartel must be able to:

1. Control a very large part of total output.
2. Have a small number of members whose dedication to higher profits overrides all other possible sources of business frictions.
3. Trade in a commodity that has:
   a. A relatively stable market
   b. An inelastic demand
   c. A price that makes substitutes uneconomic
   d. Huge capital or other requirements that make new entry into the business a very slow process.

Unless all of these conditions are met, there will be temptations for members to deviate from the cartel agreement.

Even when they have agreed to co-operate fully, it is difficult for the cartel members to choose an appropriate price. The inherent difficulties in setting the price are well illustrated by the tugs-of-war that occur several times each year between Iran, Libya and Saudi Arabia. For an artificially high price to pay off, demand for the product must be inelastic. That is, if the price is raised by a given amount, the quantity sold declines by a relatively smaller amount so that total revenue is increased by selling the smaller amount at a higher price. This means that since the total cost of production has been reduced, profits are substantially greater than they otherwise would be.

If a product is a necessity and there are no readily available substitutes, demand will be inelastic in the short run. However, a high price will cut consumption, stimulate a search for alternatives and in time the new products and, in all likelihood, the new producers will threaten the cozy position which the cartel has developed.

Although most of us only became aware of OPEC after the 1973 Middle East War, that particular oil cartel has been in existence since 1960, and it had been raising prices and taking over international oil company property for some time. Indonesia's President Sukarno in 1952 and Major Quadafi in Libya in 1969 each pushed ahead of the other members of the oil cartel in terms of both ownership and price for their product.

It was Quadafi who forced the pre-Arab-Israeli War increase in price from 85 cents to well over $3.00 a barrel. And, it was his politicizing of oil that finally embarrassed the Gulf producers into the embargo as a political tool to be used to separate Israel from her friends, and her friends from one another. Putting all the emphasis on post-October 1973 events, however, produces a distorted view of what was already happening within OPEC. If Egypt and Syria had not launched their attack on Israel in 1973, the Shah of Iran (belatedly adopting as his own the 1951 policy of Premier Mussadegh whom he had had eliminated) would have taken other steps to raise prices and buy control, and Quadafi would have found some other means for provoking hostile oil action against Israel and her friends.

Since the late 1960s OPEC has been operating under conditions which favor success in the short run. Rising living standards, growing population and increasing industrialization all over the world have combined to increase requirements for petroleum and to assure that demand stays higher than it was in 1970, even when economic activity in the industrial, oil-using countries slips. However, the cartel's price policy is stimulating exploration and development of new capacity for both oil and other energy sources in non-cartel countries, and has reversed the steady growth in the demand curve.

The current success of the oil producers in restricting output and fixing prices seems to create a tempting technique for countries with substantial production and reserves of other natural resources. The degree of concentration in eleven metallic minerals in 1973 is shown in Table 4.1.

Production of four of the materials listed above is very highly concentrated. That is, three to six countries account for from over one-half to three-quarters of the world's output (not including the United States). The small number of countries involved and the high proportion of production they account for would seem to make these materials prime targets for cartelization. Each of these is discussed separately.

Table 4.1   Concentration in Production of Eleven Metallic Minerals in 1973

Material	Major producers other than United States	Concentration of named countries' share of world production (%)
Bauxite	Australia, Jamaica, Surinam, Guyana, Guinea, Dominican Republic	68
Chromium	South Africa, Turkey, Rhodesia, Philippines	46
Copper	Canada, Chile, Zambia, Zaire, Australia, Peru, Philippines, South Africa	50
Iron Ore	Australia, Canada, Brazil, India, Sweden, Liberia, Venezuela, Chile	36
Lead	Australia, Canada, Mexico, Peru, Yugoslavia, Morocco, Sweden	41
Manganese	South Africa, Brazil, Gabon, India	42
Mercury	Spain, Italy, Mexico, Yugoslavia, Canada	56
Nickel	Canada, New Caledonia, Australia	59
Tin	Malaysia, Bolivia, Thailand, Indonesia, Australia, Zaire, Nigeria	74
Tungsten	Thailand, Bolivia, South Korea, Canada, Australia, Portugal	28
Zinc	Canada, Australia, Peru, Mexico, Japan, West Germany, Sweden	52

Tin output is concentrated in seven locations. These countries have an existing arrangement, the International Tin Agreement. The objective has been price stabilization when demand would not readily clear the market. Tight supply in the early 1970s made their pricing agreement inoperative for several years, but the depression and lower prices brought it back into operation in April 1975.

Bauxite production has almost the same degree of concentration as petroleum. However, Australia, the leader, accounts for only 28 per cent, a much smaller single share than Saudi Arabia has in the world's oil picture. The 40 per cent accounted for by Jamaica, Surinam, Guyana and the Dominican Republic (Haiti is a potential major producer*) would make this similar to the situation in oil if Australia and Guinea were in the Caribbean and shared the cultural and religious traditions of those countries. The International Bauxite Association was organized in 1974 but its members have not acted yet as a unit. The new trend

---

*By 1985, Brazil will be a major exporter.

for bauxite producers as set by Jamaica will be discussed in some detail shortly.

Nickel has so far been produced chiefly in Canada with New Caledonia and Australia gaining an important role in the last few years. Other countries that are becoming major producers are the Dominican Republic, The Philippines, Indonesia, Guatemala and Colombia. It is expected that their share of the market will expand sharply.

Mercury production is dominated by Spain and Italy. Together they account for more than half of the total (Spain alone about one-third). These two countries have long worked together on production and price policies. A broader base (measured in number of participating countries) is essential for an effective cartel. Increased supply and decreased demand led to meetings between Italy, Spain, Mexico, Algeria, Yugoslavia, Turkey and Canada in 1973 and 1974. In May 1974 they managed to agree on a floor price of $350 a flask. However, it is recognized that there is no machinery to avoid cheating or, in short, to have an effective cartel. Emphasis was shifted to promoting use of mercury and joint technical studies in April 1975. The technical and promotional activities will be conducted by a new organization officially named Assimer. Its six producing country members account for about 75 per cent of world quicksilver exports.

Other materials with high degrees of concentration present less-likely cartel potentials. Although there is a concentration of 52 per cent of the zinc production in seven countries (other than the United States), and 50 per cent of the copper output in eight, they do not appear promising for cartel action. The Intergovernmental Council of Copper Exporting Countries (CIPEC) is made up of Chile, Peru, Zambia and Zaire which account for about 30 per cent of world mine production and about half the copper entering world trade. The group now has a 15 per cent cut in production in force in an effort to clear an unwieldy surplus. There is the International Lead and Zinc Study Group established under the auspices of the United Nations which is an information collecting group and not a cartel.

The Association of Iron Ore Exporting Countries was formed in 1974, but several substantial shippers have not yet joined. The developing world's largest exporters of iron ore are Algeria, Brazil, Chile, India, Liberia and Venezuela, and together they account for 18 per cent of world production. Australia, Canada and Sweden are also substantial exporters.

The other major materials in the list in Table 4.1 have significant degrees of concentration, but demand for them fluctuates to an even greater degree with ups and downs in business conditions. Probably more important, many of them have large backlogs of 'old' scrap that will be collected and used at high prices, and the use of substitutes for them increases as prices go up. These make the operation of a cartel not merely difficult, but practically impossible.

There are other major obstacles to cartelization: (i) co-operation among customers or users to break artifically high prices, and (ii) the stimulus to new investment in exploration, development and production of not only the basic material but also of actual and potential substitutes for it. These difficulties do not mean that cartels will not be formed. New ones are being organized and once the depression is over, more will be.

Jamaica : A New Trend in Cartelization

It is tempting to compare the bauxite situation to that in oil. While bauxite-producing countries would welcome an organization as strong as OPEC, it is not likely that they ever will have that kind of clout.

Known and proven oil reserves are limited and this fact gives producing countries great power. But bauxite, named after the French town, Les Baux, from which the raw material came in the beginning of the industry, is the world's most plentiful metal ore. The bauxite group must reckon with this fact, as well as the reality that there are exporters who do not belong to the International Bauxite Association. The ones that have come together are Australia, The Dominican Republic, Guinea, Guyana, Jamaica, Sierra Leone, Surinam and Yugoslavia.

This lumps together four continents, several races and a variety of political ideologies. The one thing they have in common is a desire to harmonize policies on bauxite. This led Jamaica to believe that other important producers would not undercut her when she broke off negotiations with six aluminum companies in May 1974, and unilaterally increased bauxite taxes and royalties by more than 700 per cent.

Two companies, Kaiser and Reynolds, mine raw bauxite in Jamaica and ship it to refining plants in the United States. Four others mine bauxite, refine it into alumina on the Island and ship the powdery white substance to smelters in the United States, Canada and Europe to be turned into ingot. These companies are Alcoa, Alcan, Revere and Alpart, the last a consortium of Reynolds, Kaiser and Anaconda. Alcan Aluminium Limited is Canadian–the others are United States Companies. Jamaica has completed the acquisition of 51 per cent of Kaiser's and

Reynold's holdings in the Island and is negotiating to acquire 51 per cent of the Jamaican operations in each of the four others.

Several of the companies claim their original agreements with Jamaica prohibit unilateral action on taxes and royalties by the government. They have taken the issue to the World Bank's International Center for settlement of investment disputes. A part of the current negotiations between the companies and the government involves the action already in arbitration. The Jamaican Government has insisted it will not be bound by any decision taken through the Bank for International Development's Arbitration.

The companies' long-term position with respect to Jamaican bauxite as well as other third-world governments and their methods of controlling natural resources was probably best put by the chairman of the board of Alcoa, Mr. Harper. After the controversial Jamaica tax increase went into effect, he said, 'If a sovereign government chooses to violate the contract that protects our investment, does it make good sense to expand our operations in that country? Obviously, it doesn't.' The question for the long term then will be whether or not Jamaica can make it in bauxite on its own.

The drive behind the Island Government's 1974 action was a need to do something about its economy. There was nothing new about that, but the dual impact of OPEC action on the balance of trade made matters worse. The fourfold increase in the price of oil first increased costs not only for energy, but also for agricultural operations and the Island's small industries. Then it hit tourism which figured prominently on the plus side of the balance of payments.

It was really not too surprising, therefore, that the government would demand more revenue from its major asset, bauxite, as well as more control over it. It is assumed that ownership of bauxite company holdings will increase the Island's income and provide the means of raising the gross national product. Jamaica has long been burdened with a high rate of unemployment and even today has a *per capita* income of only $600 a year.

Viewed from the other side, the Jamaican tax on the 344 pounds of bauxite required to make the 80 pounds of aluminum in a new American automobile runs around $2. On an American mobile home the new levy amounts to something like $20. Tributes of less than a dollar are contained in consumer items like step-ladders, and pots and pans, and only pennies in foil for cooking and wrapping.

In addition there is the tribute aluminum must pay to OPEC

for higher energy costs to be included in the price of aluminum ingot. Since the process is energy-intensive, this amounts to 10 per cent or more to be included in the base price against which the Jamaica levy is measured.

Cartel, International Commodity Agreement, or?

Although Jamaica's action on bauxite has produced a cartel-like result, it may or may not turn out to be another OPEC. We will predict that The International Bauxite Association will not become a BAUPEC. And, we very much doubt the likelihood of success for the other basic commodity organizations unless and until we again have prosperity like that of the early 1970s.

What is likely to happen is demonstrated by the situation that has developed in coffee. The Inter-American Coffee Agreement of 1940 was expanded and revised, and continued in effect until 1973. The reason–coffee production has usually been greater than consumption. This relationship changes from time to time, as it did when consumption expanded sharply from the end of World War II into the early 1950s. Another shift to more consumption than production took place in 1967 and by 1973 prices for coffee were almost equal to post-World War II highs.

This price situation led Angola, Brazil, Colombia and the Ivory Coast, which together produce some 60 per cent of the world's coffee, to believe that they could go it alone. With that decision, when the then current International Coffee Agreement reached its terminal date in 1973, they chose not to seek a new one.

In mid-1974, the price of Brazilian coffee hit an all-time high in New York–80 cents a pound; Central American varieties peaked at 75 cents; and Colombian set a new record at 82 cents. That was in a free market. Because the producers liked it that way, they felt that they had to take action to insure not only that they would get high prices but also that they could combine to get even higher ones. So, they tried to make the equivalent of an OPEC in coffee.

The four main countries set up a multinational corporation for marketing, control of production and, when necessary to hold up prices, stockpiling. The Central American exporters, backed by Venezuela's oil money, established a similar firm. It looked good until prices started to soften late in 1974. At that time, both groups agreed to hold back 20 per cent of the 1974–5 crop. But withholding production that had worked for oil prices fell apart in coffee.

Exceptionally favorable growing conditions attended the 1974–5 crop. In addition, the high prices had led to increased

coffee cultivation which meant that the harvest would once again
be much greater than the demand. So, despite the agreement
to withhold from the market, Angolan farmers decided the revolution in Portugal meant 'sell' for them. Central American shippers
found the temptation to unload while prices were still attractive
more than they could resist.

As a result, in early 1975 Central American coffee prices
dropped to a level 8 cents below the market that had prevailed
when the International Commodity Agreement had been permitted to lapse in 1973. The coffee of the four main countries was
in much the same price position. Now all the producers are
suffering, their cartel dream is a nightmare and there is again
talk of a new International Commodity Agreement.

Although Brazil's frost and Angola's internal political problems
boosted prices sharply in the summer of 1975, the earlier drop
in prices just described did result in a new agreement. This
was an extension of the 1968 pact but without provisions for
import/export quotas. It expires September 30, 1976. The Coffee
Council composed of signatories to the agreement will meet in
London, October, 1975.

Conclusion

The coffee story is likely to describe the situation for natural
product cartels in the years immediately ahead. That is, except
for 'acts of God' like Brazil's frost and hyper-prosperity in the
industrialized countries, raw commodity producers will not be
able to boost prices by joint action. When prices drop they will
be happy to turn the whole business of price determination over
to their governments. They will welcome intergovernmental commodity agreements on the terms of the Havana Charter, since
'a reasonable degree of stability on a basis of such prices as
are fair to consumers and to provide a reasonable return to producers' would mean higher prices than those likely to prevail
in a competitive market.

That doesn't mean the cartel idea will pass into limbo. If
OPEC continues to call the tune for the industrial world, it
will remain an ideal which all one-material, one-crop
export-oriented countries will strive to follow. That will be true
even if OPEC shows signs of strain and has to yield a little
on prices. If world demand for oil continues to slump, special
price cuts like those already made by Ecuador, Libya and Abu
Dhabi, might spread. However, experience to date shows Saudi
Arabia and Iran more able to control the producers than the
United States or Europe or Japan in organizing the consumers.

We should have learned something from post-1973 experience. That is, that when, as, and if we get back to something like an annual rate of economic growth of 4 per cent or more, we will once again become potential victims for basic material cartels.

5. A World of Scarce Resources?

Natural resources become available for man's use through a lengthy and complex process. Although we start with nature's endowment of the non-renewable materials, it is only when man's knowledge, ingenuity and technological capabilities have been applied that these can be converted into usable industrial products. This transformation has been a long process. Its history demonstrates that in the short run there is not much that we can do about it when shortages are upon us. This is the most potent lesson to be learned from the scarcities of the early 1970s. It should also be the basis on which we can start to deal with the problems of future scarcity in natural resources. Policy at all levels, both private and public, must recognize the long-term nature of the problem and the need for continuing, rather than *ad hoc*, means for dealing with it.

The nature of scarcity is crucial to an understanding of the natural resources problem. Practically all materials are scarce under most circumstances in the sense that, if they were available without cost, more would be demanded than could be supplied. The counterpart of pervasive scarcity is the unlimited extent of man's material wants. The overwhelming majority of the world's population always want a little more income, sometimes a lot more, almost without regard to the current level of its well-being.

Scarcities obviously can be the result of either too small a supply or too great a demand. Although it may be obvious, establishing this relationship is not the simple and straightforward one some might think it to be.

A great many different methods are used in both the forecasting of the demand for, and the estimating of the supply of, basic materials. At the present time there are no standardized techniques for making either long-term demand projections or estimates of resources availability. Probably equally important, we have no means available today to meaningfully assess the adequacies or accuracies of existing data.

On the supply side, part of the problem originates in the proprietary and international nature of many aspects of the extractive businesses. On the demand side there is the inherent problem of adequately estimating the GNP and then converting whichever GNP figure is arrived at into terms of specific material requirements. Many efforts to fill this need have been made often, but so far none of them have been successful.

Although we know that all historic projections of scarcity have turned out to be wrong, there is no gainsaying the fact that ultimately there is a limit to both the earth's crust and its content of available material. In the long run, non-renewable resources like minerals and fossil fuels are scarce in the same sense that Rembrandt paintings, Hester Bateman silver, and other works of art are one-of-a-kind. It is for this reason that the doomsday prophets command our attention from time to time. Obviously their views on the availability of non-renewable resources are worth listening to. That is particularly true if it stimulates the thinking and action necessary to prove such prophecy unfounded.

Calculating Supply

Information on world stocks of natural resources is inadequate even for the major metals and non-metallic materials. It is obvious, therefore, that we cannot make an assessment of the world's resources with any degree of accuracy. Working from the published estimates, a tabulation can be put together for the industrialized nations and the developing countries and these data are shown in Table 5.1.

In some interpretations, reserves, particularly the proven reserves of major materials, may not seem very large. However, in the long run, we have reason to be sure that technological progress will make it possible to extract the essential materials from any kind of rock or clay. For example, 100 tons of granite* contains 8 tons of aluminum, 5 tons of iron, 1,200 pounds of titanium, 175 pounds of manganese, etc. In the not too distant future, therefore, improved techniques for processing low-grade ores can provide very large additional supplies. To that possibility we can also add the likelihood of more extensive recycling of today's mineral waste.

---

*Including the kind used in memorials to the dead but, for the most part, the unstratified igneous rock which is one of the most abundant materials in the earth's crust.

Table 5.1 Availability and Source of Major Mineral Resources

Metallic Ores	Amounts estimated in 1972 (Millions of Tonnes)	Main Countries
Iron	232,000 (64,000 known)	Australia, Brazil, Canada, Chile, India, France, Norway, Sweden, United Kingdom, United States
Manganese	1,014 (403 proved and probable)	Brazil, Gabon, India, Republic of South Africa
Titanium	659.6 (more than 50 per cent is difficult to dress)	Australia, Canada, India, Republic of South Africa, Norway, United States. New deposits have been discovered and are being worked in Australia, Cameroon, Malaysia, Mozambique, New Zealand and elsewhere
Chromium	1,451	Iran, Malagasy Republic, Philippines, Rhodesia, Republic of South Africa, Turkey
Nickel	72.16 (31.3 proved and probable)	Australia, Canada, Colombia, Indonesia, New Caledonia, Philippines, Venezuela
Molybdenum	5.2 (3.5 proved and probable)	Canada, Chile, Greenland, Mexico, Peru, United States
Copper	334 (203 proved and probable)	Canada, Chile, Peru, United States, Zambia. New deposits have been discovered in Australia, Guatemala, Iran, Japan, Philippines and elsewhere
Lead	100.8 (61.1 proved and probable)	Australia, Canada, Mexico, Peru, United States. New deposits have been discovered in Japan and elsewhere
Zinc	150.4 (94.6 proved and probable)	Australia, Canada, Federal Republic of Germany, Japan, Mexico, Peru, United States
Tin	7.1 (2.9 proved and probable)	Australia, Bolivia, Burma, Indonesia, Malaysia, Nigeria, Thailand. New deposits have been discovered in Brazil, Namibia, Zaire

Aluminum (Bauxite)	9,500 (3,500 proved and probable)	Australia, France, Ghana, Guinea, Indonesia, Jamaica, Malaysia, Sierra Leone, Surinam
Mercury	0.498 (the majority in monometallic mercury deposits)	Canada, Italy, Mexico, Spain, United States
Gold	35–40	Australia, Canada, Ghana, Philippines, Republic of South Africa, United States
Metals of the Platinum group	6,966	Canada, France, Republic of South Africa, United States
Uranium	1,039	Canada, France, Republic of South Africa, United States
Silver	270–300 (150–170 proven and probable)	Australia, Canada, Mexico, Peru, United States
Potash	63,000	Canada, France, Federal Republic of Germany, Italy, Spain, United States
Sulphur	912.5	Chile, Iran, Mexico, United States
Phosphates	67,500	Algeria, Morocco, Tunisia, United States, Venezuela
Borate minerals	187.0	Argentina, Chile, Turkey, United States
Kaolin	10,040	France, Federal Republic of Germany, India, United Kingdom, United States
Graphite	157.2	Austria, Federal Republic of Germany, Republic of Korea, Malagasy Republic, Mexico
Asbestos (fiber)	96.4	Australia, Canada, Republic of South Africa, United States
Fluorspar (fluorite)	140.3	Canada, France, Italy, Namibia, Mexico, Republic of South Africa, Thailand, United Kingdom, United States
Diamonds	1.0 billions of carats	Countries in central and southern Africa, Brazil, Venezuela

Source: Laveros, M. (ed.), *The Mineral Resources of the Industrially Developed Capitalist Countries and of the Developing Countries*, Geologicheskiy Fond (Moscow, 1972). As indicated in the introduction to this table, there are no 'firm' figures. As a result, we have not attempted uniformity in this book

In addition, there are promising possibilities for extracting major quantities of minerals at depths of three to four miles in the earth's crust. New instruments and equipment are an essential first step for dealing with the intense heat and pressures encountered at these levels. But nuclear development and space vehicles both required early resolution of problems of this kind.

Then there is the sea. At the end of the Second World War, the surface of the earth was practically unknown beyond the edges of the continents. Yet nearly three-quarters of the earth's surface lies beneath the oceans. Until the last few years, geologists and geophysicists had declared this part of the world to be of little interest. Now they have found there the forces that shape the continents, create mountain ranges and cause eruptions and earthquakes, all matters that had baffled scientists for a long time. It has been said that to the earth sciences, the current situation is like that after publication of Darwin's *The Origin of Species*, or Einstein's *The Theory of Relativity*.

Recent surveys indicate that the ocean floor contains millions of tons of aluminum, copper, iron, manganese, magnesium and nickel, as well as very large quantities of other minerals. These deposits may be substantially larger than any yet discovered by prospecting on dry land. Sea-water obviously contains salt. Calculations already made indicate the availability of astronomical quantities of sodium, chlorine, magnesium, etc. Sea-water also contains cobalt, copper, molybdenum, nickel, silver and a long list of other elements. Given the appropriate conjuncture of price and technology, the resources under the oceans could multiply presently-known reserves of minerals by a magnitude.

There are other potential sources of supply. Since we already have a substantial production of synthetic minerals, it is likely that present methods for producing artificial diamonds, rubies, graphite, quartz and the like, can and will be extended into other materials. Science and technology continuously present new possibilities for the production of other synthetic materials. These provide one of the many possible solutions to the problem of replacing or augmenting natural resources that are in short supply.

Estimating Demand

On the demand side, the data are even less reliable. However, the National Commission on Materials Policy in the United States undertook one such estimate as is shown in Table 5.2.

From the Commission's calculations and other data, we can make general statements, such as it would appear that given

Table 5.2 Demand for Materials in Four Countries 1951–2000 (Unit Per Billion Dollar Gross Domestic Product)

	UNITED STATES			JAPAN		
	1951–5	*1966–9*	*2000*	*1951–5*	*1966–9*	*2000*
Crude Steel (mt million)	91	134	166	6	49	203
Iron Ore (tons million)	59	75	141	3	40	161
Copper (mt million)	1,297	1,887	4,389	97	650	2,996
Aluminum (mt 1000)	1,213	3,424	15,675	40	581	6,420
Zinc (mt 1000)	859	1,209	2,822	86	493	1,846
Fluorspar (mt 1000)	513	1,121	4,076	23	412	2,675
Sulfur (mt 1000)	5,246	8,712	26,648	1,242	2,006	7,490
Energy (coal equiv. mil. mt)	1,252	2,032	5,878	77	240	1,605

	USSR			CHINA		
	1951–5	*1966–9*	*2000*	*1951–5*	*1966–9*	*2000*
Crude Steel (mt million)	38	99	319	2	16	86
Iron Ore (tons million)	28	74	235	2	23	110
Copper (mt million	367	872	2,940	9	150	840
Aluminum (mt 1000)	286	1,183	6,552	3	133	1,056
Zinc (mt 1000)	240	471	1,470	8	133	720
Fluorspar (mt 1000)	166	495	2,604	61	149	696
Sulfur (mt 1000)	—	2,663	10,920	—	1,167	5,400
Energy (coal equiv. mil. mt)	372	948	4,032	79	346	1,536

Source: The National Commission on Materials Policy United States Government Printing Office, Washington, DC (1973)

the estimated rates of population growth and current ideas about probable changes in economic well-being, the world has a supply of coal adequate for at least the next 150–200 years. In iron, which has long been, and will remain for many years to come, 'the daily bread of industry', the situation is well within control for at least the next two centuries.

Because of technical progress, the importance of aluminum is bound to increase. Here again, although the immediate situation may seem a bit scary to some, Chapter 7 should alleviate those fears, given three factors: first, the recent history of new discoveries, second, continuing improvement in technology and processing, and third, the very real probability of substitutes– particularly synthetic ones–combine to make it unlikely that there will be a threat of real scarcity. Although there can and will be a possibility of short-term shortage until 1985, there is no reason for continuing scarcity by, let us say, 1990 or in the twenty-first and twenty-second centuries. That is if we adopt the appropriate policies now.

Data and Methodology

Economics, technology, price and policy assumptions are part of every statement made about resource demand and supply, or abundance and scarcity. So before we start building models, writing equations and developing computer programs, we shall just take a close look at what we have to work with, the existing data, and then examine the available tools, the methodologies for analysis.

The resource estimates that are now used for many, if not all, natural materials are seriously deficient as a basis for national or international planning. Although they utilize the existing state-of-the-art for calculating present-day availability, the estimates rarely (if ever) attempt to project the effects of potential improve-ments in exploration, extraction and/or processing, substitution, changes in consumers' habits, etc. That means when future avail-ability of materials is the problem, the current published and private estimates should be viewed only as a beginning. The past history they cover must then be re-evaluated and re-studied in light of the scientific, engineering, economic, social and political factors that will determine future rates of output and demand.

In attempting to deal with the natural resource problems both private and public efforts have been handicapped and in many cases rendered impotent by inadequate, inaccurate or inaccessible information. Although government, both national and inter-national, is already deeply involved in resource management, it does not now have proper information either for formulating policy or for basing action programs.

In the United States the General Accounting Office (Congress's 'Watchdog Agency') in a 1974 report called for a central agency with monitoring, analysis, and forecasting responsibilities. In our opinion such an agency would be a eunuch unless it developed an information system several magnitudes better than those now used. As I described it in a 1974 report for Senator Jackson,* this system would follow the general principles that were gradually introduced in 1940 as the basis for resource management by the American Government in World War II. That method will not be spelled out here. For those interested in following up on this idea, a detailing is available in *Wartime Industrial Statistics*.†

However, improving the data is no small task. As then Secretary of the Treasury, G. P. Schultz said about the GAO's 1974 report, adoption of such a system 'would constitute a fundamental change in the economic philosophy of this nation', and would imply that it was more desirable for the Government to make essential decisions than to leave them to a 'free, competitive and open market'. In a slightly different view of 'free, competitive and open', Dr. C. H. Madden, Chief Economist, United States Chamber of Commerce suggested that the multinational corporations should establish institutions for this purpose. More will be said about this in the next chapter since here our primary interest is in data and the methodology for analysis, rather than management methods.

The purpose of the foregoing is to say simply that the necessary data are not now available and it will be a major undertaking (both professional and political) to get it. Given reasonable data the estimating of supply would be relatively simple and the methodology for handling demand would become relatively straightforward. With the data now in use, demand analysis becomes something like picking the winners at the horse races. (As an aside, it should be noted that the race horse selector has better data than that now used for policy analysis.)

Present methodology for projecting demand stumbles and falls repeatedly over a series of hurdles that must be removed before we can have meaningful policy on the demand side. First there must be recognition that the projections for policy-making are

---

*'Resource Allocation Experience 1939–1948 and Its Application to 1975–1985 Energy Program Management' by David Novick, *Materials Shortages*, Committee on Government Operations, United States Senate, February 1975.
† *Wartime Industrial Statistics*, Novick and Steiner, University of Illinois Press, 1950.

not one immutable future. They are rather projections of a range of possibilities, spelled out as a minimum in high and low terms. The accurate forecast is the first hurdle to get over.

Second, income elasticities and price elasticity for natural resources must be handled better than has been done to date. For example, Professor Malenbaum,* University of Pennsylvania, points out that his analyses show declining intensity of use of natural resources as Gross National Product increases. He also points to income variance as a major factor in differences in total quantities used as population increases. In short, he disagrees completely with methodology and conclusions of such prestigious efforts as that of the Committee on Mineral Resources and the Environment (Comrate) sponsored by the National Academy of Sciences (United States).

Third, there is the question of what kind of model should be used if we are to have the benefit of modern technology such as computers and mathematics, and statistical techniques such as regression analysis. 'System Dynamics' has had one major round in natural resource scarcities through the work sponsored by the Club of Rome. Econometric models are widely used in forecasting and policy analysis. An ideal model for resource demand would consist of a large number of quantitative relationships covering technological, social, economic and political relationships governing materials consumption. However, such a model must be classed as visionary given the quality of data now available and the problems in making revolutionary improvements in its quality.†

Finally, there is the question of defining *demand, requirements, use* and *consumption*. To the economist, *demand* is want reinforced by ability-to-pay. To the military, *requirements* is everything the appropriate manual prescribes as required to carry out a military operation. *Use* may cover something old or something new and be either yesterday's, today's or tomorrow's demand. *Consumption* means to use up, as in putting gasoline through a combustion engine. So, defining terms may be either the first or the last hurdle to get over in dealing with natural resource demand methodology and data.

---

*Report of Panel on Demand for Fuel and Mineral Resources: A Mino⸱ity View, p. 310–6 in *Mineral Resources and the Environment*, National Academy of Sciences, Washington DC, 1975.

†Some readers may be interested in 'Mathematics: Logic, Quantity and Method' by D. Novick, *The Review of Economics and Statistics*, November 1954, pp. 357–8; also 'Discussion of Mr. Novick's Article' by Paul Samuelson, L. R. Klein, J. S. Duesenberry, J. S. Chirman, J. Tinbergen, G. D. Champernowne, R. Solow, R. Dorfman, T. C. Koopmans, S. Harris, pp. 359–86, same issue.

Is This a World of Scarce Resources?

We know that there can be shortages of all kinds of materials. Also, that the cause can be 'acts of God', exploding demand, dislocations such as war, control as in OPEC or inadequate investment in expanding facilities for increased supplies running through the whole range of activities from exploration on into processing and distribution facilities. All of these, increased demand, war, cartels and inadequate investment, are man's responsibility not nature's. And as we have seen in Table 5.1 and will see again in the separate chapters in the selected natural resources appendix, nature's bounty is sufficient to accommodate man's reasonable demands.

The materials selected for brief analysis in the appendix are good indicators of what is, has been and can be expected in the future for natural resources. Aluminum (Chapter 7) was given first place because it is the newest of the major metals. As such it shows what need, for example, aircraft for World Wars I and II, can do by way of stimulating both technology and investment. Since the wartime developments completely overshadowed the events of aluminum's earlier period, it is especially noteworthy to consider the five-fold expansion that private industry subsequently built on the foundation that government directed and paid for in the Second World War.

Timber (Chapter 8) comes next for two reasons: first, because it is the most commonly used of all of the materials; and second, because it is the only truly renewable resource. To be sure, 'renew' means twenty-five, fifty or more years but the opportunity is there. It presents an excellent illustration of the management challenge that must be met by both private and public interests.

We then turn to zinc, primarily because its use in galvanizing and brass makes it a material not commonly recognized by most people. More important, it presents a very good illustration of substitution. The most familiar one is the plastic bucket in place of the galvanized steel pails that were formerly used.

Copper is the next chapter and was selected essentially because it was man's first metal. It still holds a prominent place in materials usage as an essential element in conducting electricity and transmitting communication by telegraph, telephone, radio and television. In this second category we have already seen the technology revolution with the introduction of communication by microwave towers, satellites and other remote means of transmission instead of overhead or underground cables. It is possible that a similar technological change will develop in the movement of electrical energy from generator to point of final use to displace the miles and miles of copper wire now used.

We then go on to lead (Chapter 11) because it presents two special situations. One of these is its dissipative uses, gasoline additives and paint, which are now being outlawed as threats to health. The other is its major outlet in batteries to start motor-powered vehicles of all kinds. Here, so large a proportion of the material is reclaimed, that, short of a major innovation, there is little need for additional supplies.

Ferroalloys are discussed in Chapter 12. We chose this group rather than iron because whether it be manganese, chromium or the more recent alloying materials like beryllium and titanium, these are the vehicles of industrial and technological progress. They are the basis for precision tools and machines of all kinds. Beryllium is all-important to the airborne turbine, and titanium is indispensible in the production of 747, DC-10 and L-1011 aircraft. Without ferroalloys we would not yet be in the nuclear or space age. And it probably will be some kind of new alloy-steel that will resolve the heat and pressure problems encountered in extracting natural resources three or more miles under the earth's crust.

The final material natural resource to be considered covers fertilizer. This is because there is so much concern about future food supplies and also because, in addition to the natural potash and phosphate materials, oil and gas are major sources of fertilizer and related nutrients.

The conclusion in each of these vignettes is that there really is no scarcity in the foreseeable future or into the twenty-second century. That doesn't mean that there will not be scarcities. Although most of them, oil is the current exception, seem to have disappeared into the shrouds of the depression, they will be back at the first sign of an upturn. But, as has been said repeatedly herein, these are man-made scarcities. They are the result of: first, too little planning, private and government; second, bad or unsatisfactory data; and third, the assumption that computer programs, mathematical equations and statistics could be used as the bases for policy in place of good data and good sense.

There is no reason that we should continue to be victimized by such shortcomings. We must take a new approach to managing the problems of scarce resources. In the next chapter we will identify the lessons we should have learned from our recent and earlier experience. Using that as a base, we can then formulate the public policy and the management methods now called for.

6. What Have We Learned?

The economic destruction that we have seen since 1973 demonstrates clearly the importance of the availability and price of natural resources as a factor in mankind's welfare. Whether the change is the result of nature's or government's action, the current situation shows what can happen to the free-market mechanism when there has been too little or no long-range planning. If it were not for price and supply dislocations, the world could have all the bauxite, copper or oil that it wanted. However, as we have learned and will continue to learn from bitter experience, it is only over a period of ten, twenty or more years that it becomes possible to balance out the new relationships between supply and demand at the new prices.

Taking oil as an example, the 1973 embargo and more important, the four-fold increase in price, produced a world-wide earthquake in the business world. If there was a Richter scale for measuring economic catastrophe, the first shock, the embargo, and the second one, the price boost, would each have registered at least 8 or 9. The aftershocks, that is the inflation and depression would also have scored high. 1975s world-wide depression seems to make new tremors or quakes along the faults in the business crust that are based on bauxite, copper, manganese or other primary materials unlikely for the time being. However, it is at best a temporary stability. The threat of new supply and price shocks remains. A breath of prosperity in the air can quickly convert the presently stable situation into another upheaval.

This results from the long-term uptrend in the demand for these vital commodities that prevails through all of our economic ups and downs. Right now we are down so surplus appears. Nonetheless, a 4 per cent per year or higher growth rate world-wide or in major industrial nations would mean scarcity again. Manufacturing the products necessary to maintain a rising standard of living for an increased population means that an expanding demand for basic materials must be met. And, a steadily growing proportion of world citizenry now believes it is government duty to improve its standard of living, and somehow, no matter how, find the wherewithal to do it. This is a relatively new and different attitude.

Prior to World War I, government prided itself on the limits it placed on its sphere: armies, navies, courts and the other non-profit activities. Any idea of interfering in business was considered sacrilegious. The inter-war years, particularly the Great Depression, led industrial countries such as Britain, Germany and the United States to accept major responsibility for unemployment and public assistance. Even so, they continued to look to the private sector for economic growth and full employment. Since World War II these, too, have been accepted as government responsibility.

Although the energy crisis has forced adding it to the list of government responsibilities, the world's capitols have not yet worked out either the full significance of the situation or a meaningful policy approach. Owing to the energy crisis, the rest of the recent natural resource scarcities are now completely overlooked and are yet to be recognized as government responsibility. We will come back to a world of scarcities in a few moments. A brief look at government approach to economic growth and full employment up to 1973, will decide first how useful it can be expected to be from now to 1985 or later, when natural resources will not be available to support a 1970–3 rate of economic activity, and second, its appropriateness for later years by which time we hope the scarcities problem will have been resolved.

Government Management in the Economy

War and/or business depression have long caused governments to take a hand in managing the economy. As a minimum, it meant chucking the traditional gold standard and imposing foreign-exchange controls. That usually meant licensing and approval for both imports and exports. From there on, government interference moved upward in scope and intensity. It meant direction of manpower and output as the next steps. Occasionally it went even further: seizure of goods, confiscation of property and other measures including printing-press money and forced-loans from citizens.

As indicated, the post-World War I years brought the beginning of a new economic role for government, and the Great Depression emphasized and expanded the change. It was this evolution that led to government's present responsibility for economic growth, full employment and social welfare, policies adopted after World War II. With small modification, the ideas that developed since 1945, still prevail in the industrialized nations and have provided the *modus vivendi* of the developing countries.

Although there have been significant variations in the ways various governments have tried to implement this new policy, they have all had one tool in common—management of demand. And equally important has been the single-minded use of fiscal and monetary policy for this purpose. That is, taxes were raised, the government budget ran a surplus and the money supply was contracted in support of a policy decision to restrain the economy. In the United States, President Ford's actions in autumn 1974, and his January 1975 'State-of-the-Nation' address, taken together with the Federal Reserve Board policy well into 1975, is an excellent illustration of measures to hold back demand. Obviously if the President and his advisors had had the slightest notion of what was ahead they would not have been pooh-poohing depression in September 1974. Although the Federal Reserve Board did not print WIN* buttons, it did not sense what was happening to the economy either.

In short, government management cut back on demand at precisely the time it should have taken steps to expand it. That is not meant to be an indictment of those responsible. It is only a bold way of saying we really know very little about how to do the job.

A more detailed account of the 1973–4 events in the United States follows. In the closing days of 1973 forecasters were hedging their predictions more than usual because of the uncertain impact of the oil embargo and the associated energy crisis. Most economists believed that the American economy would grow in 1974 but more slowly than it did in 1973, with most of the rise in gross national product accounted for by price increases rather than growth in output. This was the consensus among the eleven economists assembled by the Conference Board late in 1973, and was typical of the forecasts of other leading economists.

Few (practically none) accurately predicted the extent of the actual decline. The Conference Board forecasted a rise in nominal GNP of just under 8 per cent, 5.3 per cent in prices and 2.3

---

*Whip Inflation Now, or WIN buttons, printed at President Ford's request and distributed by him until the depression made it seem silly.

per cent in real growth. Actual growth in GNP during 1974 was 6.5 per cent, a 12 per cent increase in prices and a 5 per cent decline in real output. In the same era of errors, James Meigs, then vice-president and economist for Argus Research Corporation,* projected an unemployment rate that would peak at about 5.5 per cent. The actual level of unemployment in December 1974 was 7.1 per cent of the labor force.

Most economists and businessmen were forecasting a slowdown rather than a recession for 1974. Projections made in March for the second half of 1974 continued to substantially overestimate growth in the economy. Wharton† economists had one of the gloomiest views, but still understated price increases and overstated real economic growth by substantial margins. According to Wharton, during the second half of 1974 there would be real growth of about 1 per cent. Other private forecasters were even farther off-target. Data Resources** expected a substantial dip in the first quarter real product growth, but forecasted a rise at a 1.9 per cent rate in the second quarter, and by the fourth quarter they foresaw real output rising at a 6.4 per cent annual rate.

During mid-1974 private forecasters continued to believe that real output would rise slightly and that the rate of increase in prices would slow somewhat during the remainder of the year. First National City Bank predicted a rise in the unemployment rate to possibly 6 per cent by the end of the year, with no growth in output during that period.

In early August 1974, Gerald Ford replaced Richard Nixon as President. The change in administrations appeared to give the country a psychological lift, especially since President Ford had indicated that high priority would be given to bringing inflation under control.

Despite the psychological lift, the Argus Research Corporation commented in early August that 'we now expect the consumer price index to be rising at a 10.3 per cent annual rate in the fourth quarter', instead of the 7.2 per cent forecasted earlier. Michael Evans, chief economist for Chase Econometrics†† conceded that recession 'will stay with us for the rest of the year'.

---

*A highly regarded economic advisory service, especially by Wall Street investment bankers.
†Wharton School of Business, University of Pennsylvania, operates one of the largest econometric models.
**Another business advisory service using another econometric model programmed for the computer.
††A subsidiary of Chase-Manhattan.

Even as late as mid-October, forecasters were still under-estimating inflation and overstating the level of economic activity. Herbert E. Neil, Jr., vice-president and economist at Harris Trust and Savings Bank, Chicago, forecasted an unemployment rate of 6 per cent of the work force by the end of 1974. He also predicted that automobile sales would decline sharply in the fourth quarter.

As pessimistic as most forecasters seemed to be throughout the year, they were continually more optimistic than actual events warranted. Few, if any, economists accurately estimated the declines in real output.

There were those who contended that for the most part the recession was supply-induced and that continuing inflation was due to excessive aggregate demand. These few cited the many shortage shocks to the economy which occurred during 1973 and 1974 as factors limiting the output of goods and services.

The January 1974 issue of the First National City Bank's *Monthly Economic Letter* highlighted the conflict faced by policy-makers at that time:

> To prevent inflation from making the slowdown or recession even deeper in this country, the growth of the money stock would have to be accelerated to a rate substantially higher than that of 1973. More rapid monetary expansion, to be sure, promotes and validates inflation.

The Bank's letter also pointed out that the task of the Federal Reserve was especially difficult during the cyclical currents that existed then. It contended that, historically, undue monetary expansion during recessions has proved to be the 'ultimate folly'. Also, in the short run, a recession caused by supply constraints would probably not respond to rapid growth in the money supply.

Other analysts also said the immediate downturn was due to supply problems. They viewed the accelerating inflation as the result of a strong aggregate demand pressing upon a production that was limited by shortages of many basic materials.

Early in 1974, Federal Reserve Board Chairman Arthur F. Burns presented the following analysis to the Joint Economic Committee:

> The current economic slowdown, however, does not appear to have the characteristics of a typical business recession. To date, declines in employment and production have been concentrated in specific industries and regions of the country rather than spread broadly over the economy. In some major sectors the demand for goods and services is still rising. Capital spending plans of business firms remain strong and so do inventory demands for the many materials and components in short supply.

Chairman Burns then concluded:

> A highly expansive monetary policy would do little to stimulate produc-
> tion and employment; but it would run a serious risk of rocking financial
> markets, of causing the dollar to depreciate in foreign exchange markets,
> and of intensifying our already dangerous inflationary problem.

In June, President Darryl R. Francis, Federal Reserve Bank of
St. Louis in an address at a trade association meeting, argued
that:

> . . . the economy is fundamentally very strong and there is more than
> adequate aggregate demand to promote real expansion. I view the slower
> growth in real output after the first quarter of 1973 as being attributable
> to the economy operating 'flat-out' at full capacity in an environment
> where price and wage controls severely reduced the efficiency of the
> market system in allocating resources in the production process.
>
> I do not see how the existence of wide-spread shortages of commodities
> and sharply rising prices can be viewed as characteristics of weak aggre-
> gate demand. The sharp drop in real output in the first quarter of
> this year was clearly the result of the oil boycott and related developments
> such as the truckers' strike, the allocation program, and the presence
> of controls on both prices and resource movements. Only a few industries
> were affected and all of them were energy related. Furthermore, unem-
> ployment in the first few months of this year was much smaller than
> one would have expected if the sharp drop in real output had been
> widespread and had resulted from fundamental weakness in the economy.

Chairman Arthur Burns appeared before the Joint Economic
Committee in early August and said, 'clearly, the American
economy is not being starved for funds. On the contrary, growth
of money and credit is still proceeding at a faster rate than is
consistent with general price stability over the longer term.' Based
on data available at that time, the growth of the money stock
was at a 10.9 per cent annual rate during June. According to
the Board's 'Record of Policy Actions' a major part of the step-up
was attributable to a temporary increase in foreign official deposits
arising from payments to oil exporters.

At the August meeting of the Board's Open Market Committee (FOMC), 'a staff analyst suggested that the unusually
slow pace of monetary growth in July was not likely to persist
in view of the continued sizable rate of growth in prospect for
nominal GNP; in fact, data available for early August indicated
that some strengthening had occurred already.' The range of
tolerance for M_1 and M_2 was only 2 percentage points for the
August–September period, compared with the 4 percentage point
spread for M_1 during the July-August period.

Although many of the economists at the White House Summit Conference in early September called for monetary ease, Edwin L. Dale, Jr., of the *New York Times* reported that 'high Federal Reserve officials have gone out of their way to point out, for the first time, that the Reserve's highly restrictive monetary policy has already been eased to a significant degree and they add that no "substantial" further easing is to be expected.' The money stock grew at a 1.5 per cent annual rate from June to August compared to the 6.7 per cent growth in the first half of the year. The ranges for M_1 and M_2 were 3 and $2\frac{1}{2}$ percentage points wide, respectively, for the September-October period. In November the two-month ranges of tolerance for the aggregates were somewhat higher than they were in October. Throughout the last three months of 1974, the one-month range of tolerance for the Federal funds rate was not reduced. The growth rates of both M_1 and M_2 were within the desired ranges in only one month during the second half of the year. The Federal funds rate, however, followed closely the ranges established at each meeting.

There are two, but not necessarily inconsistent, reasons for the frequent failure of the growth rates of M_1 and M_2 to be within their specified ranges in 1974. One reason was the complication of having a Federal-funds constraint as well as a monetary aggregate growth target. The other was an unanticipated change in the relationship of the growth of M_1 and M_2 to growth of the monetary base.

Few predictions, even in late 1973, indicated a 12 per cent increase in prices or an unemployment rate of over 7 per cent by the year's end. The FOMC staff did no worse of a job projecting economic activity than most other government or private forecasters. Controversies and uncertainties existed regarding the appropriate growth of monetary aggregates. Those who viewed the downturn as demand-induced recommended faster money growth while others, who viewed the recession as supply-induced and recognized the seriousness of accelerating inflation, argued for slower money growth.

In the first half of 1974 M_1 increased at a 6.7 per cent rate and M_2 at a 9.3 per cent rate. The Federal funds rate increased during the same period from 9.65 per cent in January to 11.93 per cent in June, on a monthly average basis. The growth of the monetary aggregates and the rise in the Federal funds rate were almost consistently within the ranges of tolerance specified by the FOMC.

In the second half of 1974 the rates of growth for M_1 and

M_2 were 3.9 and 6.5 per cent respectively. The Federal funds rate fell from 11.93 in June to an average of 8.53 per cent in December. The growth rates of the monetary aggregates were, for the most part, well below the FOMC two-month ranges of tolerance, while the Federal funds rate again was almost always within the specified ranges.

Even in retrospect, analysts are uncertain as to how to evaluate the monetary policy that was followed that year. Such an evaluation depends on the measure used as an indicator of the influence of policy on the economy. Those who believe that the Federal funds rate is a good indicator, concluded, that for 1974, the thrust of policy was restrictive in the first half, but less so in the second half. On the other hand, those who use growth of money as an indicator would conclude that monetary actions were expansionary in the first half and restrictive in the second.*

Some would like to say that 1974 was unlike any previous year. Just because inflation and recession both became more severe than anyone foresaw early in the year, they reason that external forces rather than their own econometric models and analyses were the culprits. The same kind of reasoning is used to explain why, even at the beginning of 1975 they did not yet see the Big Dip or depression already in progress. 1974–5 is not the first time the demand-management system has not worked too well. It took World War II to get the 1930s employment figures up to reasonable levels. In the United States, the number of unemployed was uncomfortably high once again in 1957 as well as in 1971. And, although the American economy boomed its way out of the 1969–70 slump, unemployment at 5.9 per cent in 1971 and 5.6 per cent in 1973 was among the early warning signs that there was trouble ahead.

The strains and groans in business in the early 1970s were the result of an unexpected and surprising shortage in many basic commodities. As stated in Chapter 1, 'even before the 1973–4 energy crunch, the shortage of materials syndrome had characterized the problems of doing business for a year and more.' Also, that, although it sounds strange today, as late as September 1974, the President of the National Association of Purchasing Management (United States) said, 'now, it's the buyers who are out on the road visiting vendors. We're running up fat expense accounts so we can assure our companies a steady flow of raw materials.'

---

*Susan R. Roesch, 'The FOMC in 1974: Monetary Policy During Economic Uncertainty', in *Review*, Federal Reserve Bank of St. Louis, April 1975, provided major inputs for the 1973–4 overview presented here.

From that it becomes obvious that demand-management had produced effective wants in the early 1970s, that is desire plus the money to satisfy it, in excess of goods available. And the failure to keep demand at manageable levels was equally the result of unsatisfactory supply management, or lack of management by business and government.

Private Management of Scarcity in the United States

It was not just the Yom Kippur War or the oil situation that created the shortages. Lots of raw materials were scarce by October 1973. And scarcity usually means higher prices. This encourages the filling of future needs right now. That leads to speculation, hoarding, and in the end, sky-rocketing prices.

The synergistic effect of all of these occurring at one time was to make both the raw materials and economic situations deteriorate further and faster than would otherwise have happened. Business had turned down by October 1973 after a marked slowing earlier that year. For the next twelve months, until the autumn of 1974, activity continued at a fairly high level because of the distorted price-and-supply expectations that had prevailed for several years and which led to a 1973–4 hoarding spree.

Inventories rose very rapidly during the latter part of 1973 and continued to climb throughout 1974. Stocks became burdensome late in that year as sales first stagnated and then dropped. As businessmen tried to squeeze their inventories into line with their lower sales expectations, they cut production in order to trim finished goods stocks. They then cut or cancelled orders from their vendors to slash their unwieldy stockpiles of materials.

At that point, it became clear that although both businessmen and government officials thought they knew how to manage the economy, something had gone wrong again. Although it was easier to place the blame on the Arabs for their sudden economic unscrupulousness and political recklessness, that was hardly the whole of it. Neither was the dwindling of global reserves of petroleum to the thirty or so year end-point that some citizens were concerned about. Nor was it the super-religiosity of the Moslem-Arab world.

The conditions that made the oil crisis possible were first, the sharp increase in demand that began in 1960 and really exploded in the early 1970s; second, the failure of the industrialized nations to recognize the significance of the role that petroleum played in their economic growth; and, third, taking for granted steadily increasing imports from the Middle East. It was this last, dependence on Arab oil, that made the OAPEC embargo possible and gave OPEC the power to put in a four-fold price increase.

It was also this dependence on Arab oil that businessmen and governments in the importing countries had been looking at for a decade and doing nothing about. Well, perhaps that is not quite fair! The charts for the steadily climbing demand were drawn. In the United States for example, domestic production was the flat or slipping bottom line, and expanding demand was the top climbing one. Noting the growing gap between the two lines on the charts, something was done about it: 'Imports' in large block letters was printed on the ever-widening gap.

Back to Public Management in the United States

Printing large block letters on a chart is not exactly our idea of management. Nonetheless, it becomes easier to understand that action when we look at the time dimensions and tools being used for demand management and compare them with the ones required to handle supply. The demand kit of tools is made up of government spending, tax rates and monetary aggregates. Up and down movements in these are used to stimulate or retard economic activity over periods of from several months to a year or so.

Federal Reserve Board Chairman Arthur Burns described it best in his 1975 testimony to the Senate Banking Committee. He said, 'The Fed's targets are laid out for a "long year" and subject to wide variations on a month to month basis.' And in other ways he indicated how truly short-term the monetary part of the demand management program is.

That kind of time horizon in and of itself rendered impotent the study groups to deal with the oil supply management problem. As indicated frequently in the earlier chapters, natural resource supply expansion takes decades. It is truly long range in contrast to the short-term programs that can be used on the demand side.

The present vacuum in supply management theory does not arise from a lack of talk about the need for natural resource planning or study groups and commissions. Using the United States as an example, this country has a long list of natural resource study activities. Some go back to the early conservation era of 'Teddy' Roosevelt. Franklin D. Roosevelt's 'New Deal' included a National Resources Planning Board. The post-Pearl Harbor, War Production Board was a monumental exercise in resource supply management.

The National Security Act of 1947 created a National Security

Resources Board and made it the heir to WPB's responsibility. Even with NSRB in place, on 22 January 1951 President Truman established the President's Materials Policy Commission 'to study the broader and longer range aspects of the Nation's materials problems as distinct from the immediate defense needs'. The Commission transmitted its report on 2 June 1952. Although most of its findings merit re-reading and reproduction here, we will have to be content with just an occasional quotation. The opening sentence of the report read:*

> The question, has the United States of America the material means to sustain its civilization? would never have occurred to the men who brought this Nation into greatness as the twentieth century dawned. But with the twentieth century half gone by, the question presses and the answers are not glib.

Several paragraphs later, they said:

> Today in thinking of expansion programs, full employment, new plants, or the design of a radical new turbine blade, too many of us blankly forget to look back to the mine, the land, the forest: the sources upon which we absolutely depend . . . we think about materials resources last, not first.

> Today, throughout the industrial world . . . the consumption of almost all materials is expanding at compound rates and is thus pressing harder and harder against resources . . . This materials problem is thus not the kind of 'shortage' problem, local and transient, which in the past has found its solution in price changes which have brought demand and supply into balance . . .

> The intensity of the problem arises from the convergence of powerful historical forces.

The report set out two of them and then continued with:

> A third lies in the rising ambitions of the resource-rich but less developed nations, especially of former colonial status, which focus on industrialization rather than materials export. [We omit the fourth.]

> Finally, there lingers from the Great Depression a world-wide fear of future market instability and possible collapse, which dampens the willingness of private investors and resource-rich countries to develop resources.

Although the tables and charts are different in the reports prepared under the auspices of the Twentieth Century Fund, Resources for the Future, The Club of Rome and numerous

---

A Report to the President by the President's Materials Policy Commission, United States Government Printing Office (1952) pp. 1 and 2.

other private and public organizations, all of them say the same things that were in that 1952 report. Probably the best way to describe those studies would be to say, 'They gave a report. Nobody listened.'

Turn to the Future

History would lead us to view this book you are now reading as a futile effort, too, if there had not been an energy crisis. In an article of mine which appeared in the *New York Times*, 2 December 1973, I wrote:

> The last few weeks have made all of us acutely conscious of the energy crisis. To some extent this is viewed as the heads of the Arab states wreaking vegeance on those poor Westerners who supported the Israelis.
> In this, we have concentrated our attention on petroleum because for the last few years we have been increasingly concerned about ecology. That has now been quickly converted into concern about energy, with no recognition of the fact that energy is only one of a large number of increasingly scarce natural resources.
> There has been some writing about the scarcity of commodities but no real recognition of the extent to which natural resources, whether timber, aluminum, copper or any of the other numerous foundations of an industrial economy, were getting to be in short supply.
> If the Arab sheiks opened their oil taps to the maximum, the problem would not be confronting us in real form until 1977 or 1980. The action of the Middle Eastern oil producers may be a blessing. That is, it will awaken us to the fact that ten million automobiles a year in the 1975, 1976 and possibly 1977 models would not only consume gasoline but their production would use up a variety of materials that are becoming scarcer every day. The same thing goes for air-conditioners and a wide variety of other energy-driven gadgets.
> At the root of this confrontation is not just the Arabs' reduction of our supply but also a failure of our own national resource planning. Since we have been forced to face up to the energy problem, we may now be able to work out a balance in terms of a reduced supply of energy and a dwindling supply of most of our other raw materials.
> The good old days have been slipping away while we were enjoying our hyperprosperity. Let us now prepare to be a prosperous and as comfortable as will be possible. In doing this we must realize that we have gone over the top. We have moved from plenty to scarcity.
> Belatedly, the Arab sheiks may have forced us to become wise men.

There is as yet no indication that we are acting or are about to act like wise men. Although, energy has been the subject of intensive and extended discussion in national assemblies and at international conferences, definitive action still remains the province of OAPEC and OPEC. There are calls for action on other raw materials but neither the exporters nor their industrial nation customers seem able to establish a *modus vivendi* let alone a basis for operations.

To sum up, government management of natural resources supply cannot be called a failure. The reason being that except in times of war, or for national security reasons in times of peace, government has done little or nothing about it. Instead, it has left the job to private enterprise.

And business, mindful of its duty to its investors, the realities of market instability and possible collapse as well as the impact of possible future government regulatory action, has not always pushed on in expanding supply. To be sure we have had the Guggenheim and similar investments in Chile, DeBeers in Africa, the big oil companies in the Middle East and so on. Although the list of business investments is an impressive one it only demonstrates one thing. Their programs did not provide enough raw materials to fill the demands of the early 1970s and there will not be enough to support that level of economic activity again until something not yet proposed is done on the supply side. As has been emphasized throughout this book, this can only happen by 1985 or so if government acts vigorously right now!

'New Era' Planning Activities in the United States

Interestingly enough, although the major businesses have long objected to government planning, the 1975 depression, just like the one in the 1930s, has created a new atmosphere amongst the giant corporations. Big business (at least part of it) is now talking about the need for centralized economic planning.

Robert V. Roosa, partner in the investment banking house of Brown Brothers, Harriman & Company has put it this way:

> We can't any longer afford the waste of a wholly unplanned, nor sporadic and partially planned use of resources. The time has come to develop a truly home-grown, American form of national economic planning.

Roosa was one of those speaking for the Initiative Committee for National Economic Planning. Their proposal brought out a substantial voice in their support, a slightly less loud one in opposition.

The negative reaction was stated most clearly by the Chairman of Citicorp (First National City Bank, New York City, etc.) Walter B. Wriston:

> If proponents of centralized planning came out bluntly and said they were building an economic police state, their cause would never get off the ground. The application of force, once centralized planning is

in motion, is foreordained because no plan that contains thousands of parts can possibly be agreed upon by a majority of the people.

And a hundred or so words later:

> Since, by definition the elements of the plan cannot represent the will of the majority, it then follows that the people must be taught that the will of the planner is for their own good.

Newsweek (5 May 1975) that carried Wriston's views as their 'my turn' page, captioned the statement 'An Economic Police State'. Many businessmen, academicians, politicians, media persons and other citizens would concur in both *Newsweek's* headline and Wriston's views. A larger number, substantially larger, we believe are more likely to share the position put forth by Roosa.

Hardly a day passed in 1975 without someone advancing a new proposal for national planning in the United States. The one that has shared the spotlight with the labor-business-academe proposal of the Initiative Committee for National Economic Planning was the one in amendments to the Employment Act of 1946 put forth by Senators Humphrey and Javits. In a sense, the 1946 Act called for long-range economic planning for the country. However, somewhere between the Council of Economic Advisers in the Executive Office of the President and the Congressional Joint Economic Committee, long range was lost and short run got the emphasis. The Senators' Bill would make long-range economic planning explicit and necessary.

The year 1946 was the time of not only the Employment Act in the United States, but also the Plan of Modernization in France. Under it there have been six five-year plans and the French will launch their seventh in 1976. Four concepts have been used in various combinations in the French Planification. These were to set out:

1. Conditions for full employment with stable prices, and a satisfactory balance in foreign payments.
2. Growth required in various industries and geographic regions.
3. Major problem situations in all-pervasive industries, for example, energy and transport of goods and people.
4. Choices in ways for future use of an expanded GNP.

Possibly the best characterization of the French concept was provided by M. Pierre Massé, long-time President of the Commission, in his statement, 'The Plan is less than imperative but more than indicative.' The subtle shift from indicative to imperative becomes apparent when a French firm seeks new or continued financing from the government-controlled banks.

Lack of recognition of the force of this last prod has led to more than what we believe appropriate, emphasis on the 'indicative' and enthusiasm for what seems more like guidelines rather than direction. This leads to an idea that there can be general *laissez-faire* under a government plan.

The reasons for 'hands-off' by government was recently presented in the final report of the National Commission on Materials Policy (United States), June 1973, in which they state (in Chapter 9, pp. 2–3): 'The forces of the marketplace, subject to considerations of public policy, have historically served the nation well in providing sufficient supplies of materials at reasonable prices.' That idea draws nods of affirmation and applause when presented in public talks and is always included in reports of the National Academy of Sciences' Comrate, Comsat and similar committees and commissions.

A recent book takes that idea further. It would seem to want considerations of public policy transferred to big business. In *Global Reach : The Power of the Multinational Corporation,** Professors Barnet and Muller say, 'the men who run the global corporations are the first in history with the organization, technology, money and ideology to make a credible try at managing the world as an integrated unit.' The theme of their book is that knowledge is power. It goes on to say that 'government planners do not have enough knowledge about the activities of global corporations to make the crucial planning decisions for the society. Thus the managers of the corporations have become the principal planners for the society by default.'

Doubtless this statement brings nods of affirmation, too. But before joining in that chorus it is necessary to ask one question: what were the multinational corporations doing about the supply of oil and other basic materials in the 1960s? What are they doing now?

It would seem that neither the information nor the analyses of the natural resource situation are any better when done by multinational corporations than by their governments. Up to now they both have failed miserably.

On that sour note, we return to the scarcities, the reasons for them, and appropriate policy. As indicated earlier, several of the major natural resources are analysed separately in the Selected Natural Resources Appendix. Here we will simply highlight some of the information developed there and in Chapter 5.

---

*By R. J. Barnet and R. A. Muller, Simon & Schuster (1975).

Scarcities in Natural Resources

Although there were some frightened people in 1972, 1973 and most of 1974, that kind of concern about natural resource scarcities, except for oil, seems to have evaporated. We have quickly forgotten the buyers who in those years were desperately hoarding all kinds of materials. Since then, many have quit that game. Others are broke or have sharply reduced bankrolls. But we must remember that the unprecedented prosperity of 1970–3 showed that there are temporary limits to supply, even though demand seems capable of reaching the 'no-limit' stage under our present demand-management.

There is a long list of natural resources in which expansion in demand at the 1970–3 levels outran the then available supplies. Energy is only one of them. Supply has not slipped away. It just has not kept up with the demands created by an ever-higher living standard in the industrialized countries and efforts to raise the levels of well-being in the less developed ones.

Such growth has long been a major objective of practically all peoples of the world. Now that the withdrawal of some barrels of oil have revealed that the Growth God has feet of clay, we had better make sure that there is enough of the other important raw materials to hold future economic growth together, once the energy problem is under control.

In the long run, progress in exploration will lead to the discovery of new supplies, technological advances will make more materials available from existing sources and new inventions will create substitutes for or make unnecessary many of today's critical materials that are in short supply. But regardless of long-run developments, for the next decade or so, the world's natural resources are not adequately developed to meet needs at the early-1970s requirements rates. And unless meaningful programs are put into motion in the next few years, the United States and the other industrialized nations will share shortages in a world of scarcity until the turn of the twenty-first century.

The general business climate for the next decade will be different in many ways from that which we have enjoyed for the last twenty years, particularly the part that was the super-boom. The changes will present many challenges to business and government since a lower level of business activity will be around for some time. Every recovery movement on the charts will quickly be erased by shortages.

Unless Saudi Arabia decides that it is in its interest to empty its oil basin by 1990 or so, growth rates like those of the recent past cannot be available again until 1985 or later. The emphasis on Saudi Arabia is because of her dominant position in the world's proven reserves of oil and because some other countries such as Iran have already decided that if they can get high enough prices they are willing to use up their known reserves. The year 1985 or later is set by the time required to introduce new alternatives, such as coal for oil, the even later dates for shale processing on a commercial basis, plus the relatively small additions to total supply that will come from Alaska, and the North Sea.

For the industrialized nations getting free from dependence on foreign sources means costs both in terms of resources used for expanding supply, and a new and higher price for a Btu of energy. The thing that is obvious is that *per capita* energy consumption must be reduced by specific policy and action instead of by the random selection of a depressed economy.

We know that 1975 and the years immediately after it will be poorer ones than 1972, 1973 or even 1974 in the United States, the Common Market countries and Japan. Since all these countries went up at the same time to produce the hyper-prosperity that ended in 1974, when they all stopped growing at the same time, the opposite condition occurred. The only bright spot in this picture is that the downturn in business has delayed the crisis in many other raw materials scarcities.

The hyper-prosperity that we had been enjoying, and its attendant phenomenal rate of economic growth, had meant using up mineral, timber and many other resources much more rapidly than we were replacing them. When we break the energy bottleneck and get back into a growth economy, the increasing scarcity of a number of other materials will immediately overtake us.

Aluminum, copper, steel-alloying materials, timber are some of the problem areas. For example, in the United States the copper situation is much like that in petroleum, large American supplies but when demand skyrockets there is a gap to be filled by imports. Aluminum presents a reverse of that. As there is no significant American commercially-priced supply of bauxite, more than 90 per cent of the bauxite and alumina come from Jamaica and Australia (for the future add Brazil). Manganese, chromite and ferro-alloys are in the aluminum class. Timber, a renewable resource, is in a different kind of situation.

This means that prosperity runs into temporary physical constraints in a large number of raw materials. And unless national programs for developing additional sources, as well as conservation and substitution programs are started right now, the industrialized nations will not be able to support economic growth at the early 1970s rate again even when they resolve the energy problem.

Policy Based on Past Experience

It should be obvious by now that there is only one reason for natural resource scarcity, which is failure to do the required reckoning, to formulate a positive policy and then take the action the policy calls for. That is exactly what we have *not* been doing, and many people believe strongly that it should not be done. Their logic is that it will require government to formulate, promulgate and direct that certain actions be taken, but this will interfere with the free forces of the market. As though scarcity in itself did not interfere with a free market and upset prosperous economies.

We would all like to get back to the 'good old days'. If that means economic growth and steadily improving living standards, it is not all that difficult. It simply means doing the required reckoning. Formulating positive policy and taking the actions called for. Some of you may have been non-plussed by our call for management similar to that which President Franklin D. Roosevelt used, first to meet the exigencies of depression, and then to deal with the developing and actual problems of World War II.

Our statement: 'Although there are no big bangs from guns and rockets, no visible enemy, the crisis is one of wartime proportions.' Those words coupled with the sentence a few pages later: 'The relations of government-business-private individual must be on the same basis as in 1942–5,' brought cries of alarm. Readers of early drafts of those sections in London, Washington and New York divided almost equally into two schools. One said, 'Right-on', the other shouted, 'Do you want to start a war!'

It should be obvious by now that all we are proposing is a way of avoiding war as well as minimizing the impact of the current and following economic downturns or depressions. It should be obvious, also, that we favor something like the French planning. Its indicative translated into imperative by financial and other government pressures is good enough for five-year plans.

But even the French look beyond the fifth year. And, in natural resource supply planning, ten years is a minimum. Twenty plus years is a more appropriate time-frame in which to project the final outcome when subject to the kinds of uncertainties that business can only undertake when the potential profits are so great as to warrant the gamble. Note our use of gamble rather than investment to indicate the nature of the risk in a period in which OPEC, Uganda, Mrs. Ghandi and similar upsets are almost daily events.

Our emphasis on lead-time and long periods of time may have confused some readers and annoyed others. In June 1975 Robert C. Seamans, Jr., Administrator of the new American Energy Research and Development Administration made a statement that puts technological change into a more understandable perspective. He said that the United States on two previous occasions had changed its source of energy supplies. The first time it was from wood to coal, and the second, from coal to oil. He emphasized the fact that each time the change took place over a sixty-year period.

Sixty years is a long time. Fortunately that as well as the balance of what he had to say made sense. It was a most refreshing new breeze in the hot air about energy to come from the President, Congress, the Interior Department, Oil Policy Committee and FEA for instance. But research and development is only one piece of the energy jigsaw puzzle and, as yet, there is no fresh wind blowing on the natural resource puzzles. It is another one of those times when man spends his time hoping rather than doing. There is nothing new in that. We always seem to expect someone else to find the way out for us.

When this analysis is in print, OPEC either will or will not have put another price boost in force.

If they have, and it amounts to something like the $2–$3 a barrel talked about now, all we can say is: 'Here we go again!' The only sunshine we can see in that kind of situation is that maybe this time something meaningful will be done on the policy front. We have not acted like wise men since the first blow-up. Will we now respond wisely to this second major explosion in the natural resources war? We probably would not be in a position to do anything if there is a third catastrophe.

We should all know by now that even though we are not engaged in man-to-man combat, the economic, social and political impact of the natural resource conflict that began in 1970, may be as devastating, or even more disastrous than hostilities under a declaration of war.

Selected Natural Resources Appendix

7. Aluminum

BY MARY B. NOVICK

Living in a world of scarcities we must look both forward to ask, 'Are there limits to growth?' and backwards so as to obtain from experience a basis for better estimating what the future can be expected to provide. Aluminum is an excellent vehicle for both looking at the history of one natural resource and making calculations for the future, not only in terms of a single material but also for the whole materials' world.

So we will take a close look at the magical performance by which a new material that was a rich man's curiosity even at the end of the nineteenth century became something important in the twentieth century, and the way in which it climbed into second place in the rank of all metals in recent years.

For perspective, we shall highlight some of these developments. In 1890 total world production of primary aluminum was 180 metric tons. By the turn of the century, the figure stood at 7,300 tons. The impetus of World War I brought a marked increase from 69,000 in 1914 to 135,000 at the end of the conflict. The prosperity of the 1920s saw a production peak of 267,000 tons in 1929.

The stimulus of military demands in general, and aircraft in particular, brought production in the 1930s from a beginning point of less than 220,000 tons to almost 500,000 by 1939. This new figure was dominated by sharp expansion in Canada, Germany, the USSR, Japan and the United States. It is noteworthy that Japan, whose first recorded output was 4,000 tons in 1935 expanded rapidly to an annual average of over 12,000 in the next five years, and managed to turn out 78,000 tons a year in the 1940-5 period.

As striking as is the performance of Japan, that of Germany practically matches it. It went from 70,000 tons in 1935 to an average of over 130,000 tons in the subsequent five years, then up to 270,000 tons a year during World War II. As part of this explosive world growth, Canada's output that was 20,000 tons in 1935 went soaring to an average of 295,000 per year during World War II. In the same way, production in the United States more than doubled – from 54,000 tons in 1935 to an average of just under 125,000 in 1935–9, and then to almost 500,000 tons per year during the war.

The post-World War II expansion of world output brought nearly 3,500,000 tons in 1955, over 7,500,000 in 1966, and about double that last figure by 1974. The details of country-by-country growth in the production of aluminum will be developed later, as will a review of price changes which were in large part the result of steadily improving technology. More important, lower prices also made possible many of the uses that now account for fifteen million tons a year of this new metal.

Probably as important as technology and the stimulus of military requirements are the changes in management methods. These will also be developed later. For the moment it is worth noting that it was huge government outlays that made possible the step function growth that occurred in both the Great War and World War II.

The story begins with a look at the technological developments. Since technology relates to the natural resource itself, we shall then turn to a review of the availability of bauxite and other aluminous materials, followed by a history of production and prices, and finally a discussion of the role of private enterprise and government in managing the development of the metal.

Technology

Aluminum's origin can be dated to 1782 when Antoine Lavoisier announced, 'It is highly probable that alumina is the oxide of a metal whose affinity for oxygen is so strong it cannot be overcome either by carbon or any other known reducing agent.' In 1807 Sir Humphrey Davy, who had earlier discovered the electrolytic method for releasing metal from its oxide, turned his attention to alumina oxide. Although his technique had been successful with sodium, potassium, and some other metals, it failed to isolate the hypothetical metal he named aluminium. That name and spelling is used everywhere in the world except in the United States.

So limited was the metallurgy of the nineteenth century that the world's most abundant mineral was only available for special memorials, jewellery and a few dental applications, that only the very rich could afford. In 1854, French scientist, Henry DeVille, substituted sodium for potassium in the reduction process of alumina oxide. His work marked the beginning of the production of aluminum 'commercially'* and a metal, which was once more valuable than gold, was a few years later being sold for $17 per pound.

In 1886 Hall, a metallurgist in Cleveland, Ohio, and Paul Louis Héroult in France, separately, but almost simultaneously, developed an electrolytic process known as the Hall-Héroult process, now used in the production of pure aluminum. Four years later an Austrian chemist, Bayer, modified the work of DeVille and carried it one step further through the invention of the cyclic process. This method became the procedure used in reducing bauxite to pure alumina oxide to which the Hall-Héroult electrolysis is then applied to isolate pure aluminum.

So by the beginning of the twentieth century man, in a relatively short span of time, had opened a new door to nature's lockers and was in a position to make available an additional natural resource for his benefit. But what was to ensue was not all that simple. Man's ingenuity continued to be needed to determine the properties of this new material and how to shape, form and fabricate it. Only then were its uses for commercial purposes fairly well assured. Again in another, even shorter period of time, aluminum became a general-purpose metal and the foundation of the new industry, aviation. Later, it proved useful in a number of new specialities ranging from foil for wrapping and packaging, to heavy structural sections for buildings, spans for bridges, as well as in automobiles, housing and mobile homes.

This is a good illustration of how an old natural resource became one of our most important materials, and it is an example of events that will occur over and over to free mankind from 'limits to growth'.

Today's second most important metal was a scientific concept until late in the nineteenth century, and really did not become industrially important until World War I. Even that seems an overstatement since an annual average output of less than 100,000 tons per year between 1914 and 1919 is not much compared to around 15,000,000 tons in 1974.

This new metal became a general purpose material in less than seventy-five years because of its unique properties. These are:

1. Lightness
2. Corrosion resistance

---

*Commercially is in quotes because $17 per pound was many times the price of general purpose materials such as steel and copper.

3. Reflectivity
4. Thermal and electric conductivity
5. Malleability
6. Non-toxicity
7. High strength when alloyed
8. Attractive appearance.

The original stimulus to develop aluminum for military purposes and in many other applications was due to its lightness relative to the weight of other metals. Alloying it enhances its strength as well as embodying other of the properties listed above. For example, alloys of density suitable for mechanical operation at high temperatures are used for internal combustion engine pistons. When they are also corrosive resistant they then are used for air frames, bridges, travelling cranes and engine crankcases.* When the alloy is an electrical conductor it finds extensive use in electric cables and other electrical fittings.

Bauxite is Abundant

Aluminum is the most abundant metallic element in the earth's crust. Bauxite, one of numerous ores containing aluminum, historically has been the most economically desirable source of alumina (aluminum oxide).†

Three key facts about the raw materials from which aluminum is produced are noteworthy.

1. Bauxite is abundant.
2. Bauxite ores vary in mineral content and often require specially designed refining facilities.
3. There are many aluminous ores, and existing technology for processing them.

The United States Bureau of Mines' current estimates of proven world reserves of bauxite are on the order of 15.5 billion tons, sufficient to supply all the world's smelters for more than 200 years at the current consumption rate. In the past, bauxite finds have exceeded the industry's growth rate. Enormous new reserves have been proven in South-east Asia, South America and Australia. Australia's known reserves alone could supply the

---

*The statue of the Angel of Christian Charity (popularly known as Eros) was made of corrosive resistant aluminum and erected in Piccadilly Circus, London in 1890. Today the insignificant corrosion that has developed gives the statue a pleasant grey patina.
† Statements by C. W. Parry, Aluminum Company of America and D. L. Bloom, Earth Sciences Inc., presented at hearings before Joint Economic Committee, Congress of the United States, 22 July 1974 were used in preparing much of the following material on aluminous resources.

entire world's aluminum smelters for more than seventy years at the current rate of use. There are untapped proven reserves in countries such as Brazil, which now ranks third in the world.

For some time now, it has been known that there were substantial deposits of bauxite in the Trombetas River Valley of Brazil. In May 1975 three of the world's aluminum giants announced that they were completing feasibility studies in co-operation with the Brazilian government. The search for aluminum in this part of Brazil was begun in the 1950s by Kaiser Aluminum. However, they did not succeed. Alcan moved in, in 1964; the exploration company of billionaire Daniel K. Ludwig in 1969; and Alcoa in 1970. These were the three that announced plans to spend more than three billion dollars in developing this new source.

New bauxite finds have been so numerous that there is no economic justification for developing all of them in the near term. Alcoa, for instance, recently terminated an exploration project in French Guiana and elected to allow options on bauxite deposits there to lapse. The quantity and quality of the French Guiana ore, and the cost of transporting it to a refining plant were not competitive in a world of abundant ore.

Most high-grade bauxite is found outside the United States. There are some deposits in Arkansas and Georgia, but they are minor compared to those in other nations. The United States now produces only about 3 per cent of the world's annual output.

Quality Variations in Ores

There are many aluminum-bearing ores. They are heterogeneous mixtures containing varying quantities of the oxides of aluminum, silicon, iron and titanium. Significant developments in refining technology are permitting the industry to economically produce alumina from lower-grade bauxites. A number of companies are working to find unconventional processes as substitutes for the Bayer bauxite-to-alumina oxide, and the Hall-Héroult alumina oxide-to-aluminum. Full commercialization of these efforts is still years away, but the potential looks brighter every year. At present, Alcoa in the United States, the Aluminum Company of Canada and Pêchiney Aluminum of France are among those active in this effort.

All of these aim at expanding the range of ores to be processed to include a number of common clays, shales and even spoil from coal. At present, these ores cannot be used because of their impurities.

There are numerous other potential sources of aluminum although bauxite has been the most economically attractive up to now. For example, the USSR has several plants that refine alumina-bearing nepheline, syenite and alunite. Poland is constructing a refining plant that will use an acid method for reducing common clay to obtain alumina.

While high-grade bauxite may run more than 50 per cent alumina oxide, many commercial refining plants are based on bauxites with an available alumina content of only 30 per cent. Experience in processing these lower grade bauxites has made ores of comparable alumina content, such as anorthosite, alunite and dawsonite, all abundant in the United States, attractive potential sources for the American aluminum industry.

The United States Bureau of Mines reports that reserves of non-bauxite alumina ores in America are virtually inexhaustible. Alcoa owns an 8,000 acre anorthosite deposit in Wyoming. It is estimated that the alumina content of this single reserve would supply the entire world's aluminum industry for seventy-five years at today's rate of consumption.

Earth Sciences, Incorporated of Golden, Colorado, in a joint venture with National Steel Corporation of Pittsburgh, Pennsylvania, and the Southwire Company of Carrolton, Georgia are seeking alumina from alunite. The primary purpose of their venture is the discovery and development of alunite deposits. Alunite is a mineral consisting of four industrial chemicals: alumina oxide, sulfuric acid, potassium sulphate, and water. The pure mineral contains 37 per cent alumina. In nature, sizeable deposits in excess of 30 per cent are very rare. The promise of this material is not high alumina content, but rather the ease of treatment. It is one of the three potential alumina sources that are not alumino-silicates, the others being bauxite and dawsonite. It is the aluminum-silicon-oxygen combination that makes other alternatives costly to process.

It might be useful to point to a disadvantage or a potential disadvantage of alunite, which is the lower grade of alumina in alunite, usually around 15 per cent. However, this may not be as much of a problem as it appears to be, since grade is only one factor in the profitability calculations. Other factors such as energy and raw material supplies, proximity to markets, uniformity of the material being processed, infrastructure requirements, and environmental considerations are equally as important as the grade factor.

The alunite situation could be like that of taconite iron ore in the United States some twenty-five years ago. Although taconite was only one-half the grade of the hematite high-grade ore, which the industry had been accustomed to, it was found that it could be processed competitively, and now taconite pellets supply a major portion of the iron ore market. Alunite in the Western United States may ultimately be to aluminum what the Southwest has been to copper, and what Minnesota, Wisconsin, and Michigan have been to iron.

There is also research on the possible use of aluminum-rich industrial waste materials as a source of alumina. Fly ash from power plants and waste from coal processing residues, called culm, are examples. The non-fuel part of some culm contains about the same percentages of alumina oxide as the bauxite now being processed in Western Australia. In some of this material, fuel values may be sufficient to provide part of the energy requirements of the refining process, a significant factor in today's world of energy shortages.

There is no question that the United States could become self-sufficient in the production of alumina from domestic aluminous ores. Such action could severely retard economic development in some bauxite-producing nations that are highly dependent on revenues from bauxite production.

A quick look at the world picture in aluminum is shown in Tables 7.1, 7.2 and 7.3. They cover the three stages in which the natural resource moves from the earth into materials for processing into end-products.

Table 7.1 Proven Reserves of Bauxite (Million Long Tons)

	1973	
	%	*Tonnage*
Australia	30.3	4,700
Guinea	22.6	3,500
Brazil	12.9	2,000
Jamaica	6.5	1,000
Greece	4.5	700
Surinam	3.2	500
Yugoslavia	2.3	350
Guyana	1.3	200
Soviet Sphere	4.0	620
of which:		
USSR	1.9	300
Hungary	1.0	150
All others	12.4	1,930
TOTAL	100.0	15,500

Source: Based on data produced by United States Bureau of Mines

Table 7.2 World-wide Bauxite Production (Thousand Short Tons)

	1973		1968–72 AVERAGE	
	%	Tonnage	%	Tonnage
Australia	22.7	17,696	17.2	10,827
Jamaica	19.7	15,344	19.6	12,350
Surinam	10.1	7,840	10.8	6,780
USSR	7.1	5,408	8.2	5,152
Guyana	5.3	4,144	7.1	4,499
W. Europe*	12.8	9,968	13.4	8,467
of which				
France	4.5	3,472	5.2	3,288
Greece	3.7	2,912	4.0	2,501
Yugoslavia	3.3	2,576	3.7	2,305
Other Soviet	4.9	3,808	4.8	3,033
Other Free World*	17.4	13,552	18.9	11,880
of which				
USA	2.7	2,118	3.3	2,101
TOTAL	100.0	77,840	100.0	62,998

Source: United States Bureau of Mines Data (published and unpublished)

Table 7.3 World-wide Alumina Production (Thousand Short Tons)

	1973		1968–72 AVERAGE	
	%	Tonnage	%	Tonnage
USA	25.7	7,100	30.1	6,857
Australia	14.5	4,000	10.6	2,407
USSR	9.4	2,600	9.7	2,220
Jamaica	9.1	2,500	7.5	1,707
Japan	6.9	1,900	6.2	1,416
Surinam	5.1	1,400	5.2	1,195
W. Europe	14.6	4,043	12.9	2,929
of which				
France	4.3	1,200	5.4	1,233
W. Germany	4.0	1,100	3.7	845
Other Soviet	4.9	1,350	4.8	1,105
Other Free World	9.8	2,707	13.0	2,964
of which				
Canada	4.5	1,250	5.2	1,185
TOTAL	100.0	27,600	100.0	22,800

Source: United States Bureau of Mines Data (published and unpublished)

Production

Output is a function of the technology which makes production possible. It also makes possible the markets which create demand (in terms of application and price). By 1890 the basic technology for producing aluminum was available. However, knowledge about fabricating the material into products was yet to be perfected. During the 1890s aluminum developed a bad reputation, partly as a result of attempts to apply it to uses for which it was not fitted, and partly because appropriate methods of working the material had not been developed.

As a result, at the beginning of this century about half the small output went into cooking utensils, and most of the balance was used by the iron and steel industry. In the early 1900s new demands developed practically every year. Among these were bicycle parts, headlight reflectors, flashlight powder and lithography. Then came electric transmission lines and automobile parts, and aluminum was on its way. World production moved up, from 7,000 metric tons in 1900 to 43,000 in 1910, and it crossed the 100,000 ton a year mark in 1916. Figure 7.1 shows the marked expansion from 1890 up to World War II. The explosive growth in output that starts in 1945 is shown in Figure 7.2.

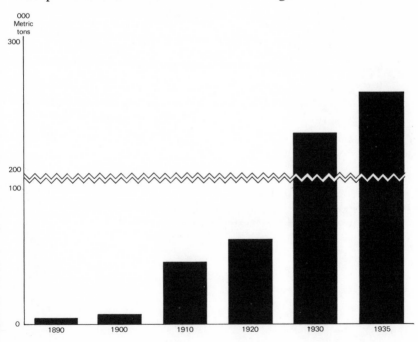

Figure 7.1 Total World Production of Aluminum 1890–1935

Today's aluminum industry can be seen as an organization carrying on four kinds of activity as shown in Figure 7.3. Bauxite is mined all over the world, usually by companies that convert it into alumina and primary products, frequently into semi-fabricated and final mill products as well as end products like foil. Chemical reduction which is carried on close to the mines is normally in the hands of mine owners. At the third

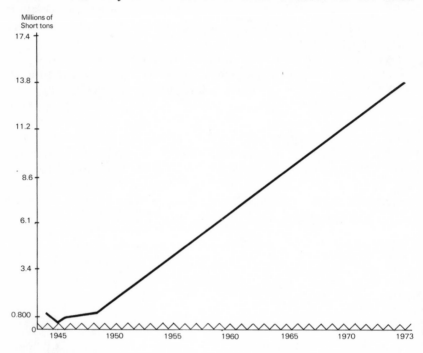

Figure 7.2   Total World Production of Aluminum 1945–1973

STEP I	STEP II	STEP III	STEP IV		
Extraction	Chemical Reduction	Primary Producer	Fabrication		
Bauxite	Alumina	Ingot	Mill Products		End products
			Semi Fabricated	Final	From foil for wrapping and cooking, on through numerous small parts and pieces, and on into cylinder blocks and heavy construction items
			1. Powder and pigment 2. Hot-rolled stock for further processing; rod, bar, wire and sheet 3. Extrusions 4. Castings	1. Cold-rolled rod, bar, plate and foil 2. Drawn and annealed wire	

Figure 7.3   Steps in Aluminum Production

Table 7.4 World Aluminum Production and Major Producing Countries:
1890–1973 (Metric Tons to 1950–Short Tons thereafter)

Year	World[1] Total	US	Canada	France	Switzerland
1890	0.18	0.3	—	0.04	0.04
1900	7.3	2.9	—	1.0	2.5
1910	43.1	15.4	3.5	9.5	8.0
1920	75.8	62.9	12.0	12.3	12.0
1930	219.0	103.9	34.0	26.0	20.5
1935	257.6	54.1	20.6	21.8	11.7
1935–9 Ave.	479.0	125.0	46.2	36.8	21.0
1940–4 Ave.	1,374.0	547.0	294.2	48.7	21.2
1950	1,644.0	719.0	396.9	66.8	21.2
1960	4,985.0	2,014.0	762.0	259.3	46.5
1970	10,641.0	3,976.0	1,072.0	420.0	101.0
1971	11,375.0	3,925.0	1,121.0	423.0	104.0
1972	12,103.0	4,122.0	1,020.0	433.0	92.0
1973	13,400.0	4,530.0	1,100.0	370.0	NA

Year	Norway	Britain	Germany	Japan	USSR[4]
1890	0	0.07	0	0	0
1900	0	0.6	0	0	0
1910	0.9	5.0	0	0	0
1920	5.6	8.0	12.0[2]	0	0
1930	24.7	14.0	30.2	0	0
1935	16.0	15.0	70.7	4.0	24.5
1935–9 Ave.	22.7	19.7	132.3	12.2	45.7
1940–4 Ave.	21.9	36.6	270.7	77.9	62.3
1950	51.9	33.0	30.7[3]	27.3	200.0
1960	181.7	32.4	186.2	146.9	745.0
1970	576.0	44.0	341.0	808.0	1,160.0
1971	584.0	131.0	471.0	985.0	1,212.0
1972	604.0	189.0	490.0	1,119.0	1,300.0
1973	670.0	NA	600.0	1,400.0	1,380.0

1. Does not equal sum of countries shown due to omission of some producers.
2. First reported production of 5,000 metric tons in 1916.
3. West Germany only.
4. First reported production of 1,000 metric tons in 1932.
Source: (1890–1935), Wallace, D. H. *Market Control in the Aluminum Industry*,
Harvard University Press, 1937 Cambridge, Mass. p. 570–71.
Yearbook of the American Bureau of Metals Statistics, American Bureau
of Metal Statistics, New York, various years

stage in which alumina goes into the 'pot' lines, separate owner-ship starts to appear. Up to this point, aluminum technology is quite different from that of other metals. In contrast, produc-tion of semi-fabricated and final mill products as well as the technology in making end products are similar to those for other metals.

The growth in world production of aluminum and in major producing countries is presented in Table 7.4. It is truly an impressive picture. It forces one to have confidence in the ability of man to convert natural resources into new materials.

Price

The first reported price for 'silver from clay' was $545 per pound in 1852. By 1855 it was $115, and in 1885, $12.00.

In 1890 a price of $3.00 a pound for small quantities was established. In half-ton lots $2.00 a pound was quoted in an attempt to widen the market. Subsequently, Hall, founder of the Pittsburgh Reduction Company wrote to a friend:*

> The mention of $2.00 in 1,000-pound lots didn't seem to interest anyone. I know a good many people look at it as a big buy, and they have reason to do so, as they know that the total consumption of aluminum in the United States has hardly been 1,000 pounds a year. People have said we didn't have 1,000 pounds. They were wrong, but they might have said, that so far as the users of aluminum were concerned, practically no one wanted 1,000 pounds.

In 1890 the output of the Pittsburgh plant was 58,000 pounds. Its production reached 1,300,000 pounds in 1896 by which time the price dropped to 75 cents. Perfections in technique, moving to hydro-electric power locations and new demands for electric wire resulted in cost reductions that translated into a price of 33 cents by 1899.

Prices have been well below that level ever since. As shown in Table 7.5, it was not until 1974 that changes in the cost of inputs like 120 per cent for bauxite and 95 per cent for fuel and power (1974 compared to 1970) brought the price back to and above the 1900 level. For the year 1974, the average was 34 cents. However, since all materials are in this same cost-push, aluminum retains its relative competitive position.

As of 4 August 1975 the New York price was 39 cents per pound with further increases promised.

---

*Edwards, Frary and Jeffries, *The Aluminum Industry*, McGraw-Hill (1930), p. 25.

Table 7.5 Average Price of Aluminum in New York (Cents per Pound in Carload Lots)

	Annual Average ($)*		*Average ($)**
		1956	0.261
1920–24	0.226	1957	0.275
1925–29	0.255	1958	0.269
1930–34	0.227	1959	0.269
1935–39	0.202	1960	0.272
1940–44	0.160	1961	0.255
1941	—	1962	0.239
1942	—	1963	0.226
1943	—	1964	0.237
1944	—	1965	0.245
1945	0.15	1966	0.245
1946	0.15	1967	0.250
1947	0.15	1968	0.256
1948	0.157	1969	0.272
1949	0.17	1970	0.287
1950	0.177	1971	0.290
1951	0.19	1972	0.265
1952	0.194	1973	0.253
1953	0.209	1974	0.341
1954	0.218		
1955	0.237		

*98–99 per cent virgin aluminum ingot in New York Open Market 1920–1933; 99 per cent pure starting in 1934, 99.5 per cent pure starting in 1953.
Source: 1920–1933, Wallace, D. H. *Market Control in the Aluminum Industry*, p. 242 1934–1974 Commodity Yearbook

Management Methods

Napoleon III's government was the first to finance the development of aluminum. He was told about the new metal and saw it as a way to lighten the weight of his armies' equipment. For this reason he granted a large sum for research on production of the new material. Military requirements were again responsible for the doubling of output in World War I. Preparations for World War II as well as actual conflict were the occasion for a tripling of production. Obviously, governments financed all of these changes. The rest of the story of aluminum's development is a glowing tribute to private enterprise.

In practical terms, Héroult, Hall and the Cowles Brothers launched the new industry. Héroult's patents were European, those of the Cowles and Hall, American. In 1887, Schweizerisch Metallurgische Gesselschaft bought rights from Héroult. By 1889, they were producing pure aluminum. Héroult, who had been working with the Swiss then returned to France and joined Electrometallurgique Francaise to help them perfect their production methods. In 1896, British Aluminum took a license from Héroult.

Hall and several financiers formed the Pittsburgh Reduction Company in 1888. Five years earlier, the Cowles Electric Smelting Company had succeeded in smelting zinc in an electric furnace. By 1885 they had successfully tackled aluminum. Shortly after the turn of the century, the Cowles Company decided to sell its patents and right to engage in the aluminum business to Hall and his associates. Their Pittsburgh Reduction Company first became American Aluminum Company. Later it divided into Alcoa and Alcan Limited, Canada.

So one Swiss, one French and two American organizations had launched aluminum on its spectacular journey. By 1914, there were one American, two Swiss, three French, one Italian and two British firms. These companies would cross national boundaries, and new ones would both start fresh or result from the reorganization of the earlier ones. Energy, ore, national military and economic goals directed investment in aluminum by both private firms and governments.

Experience in the United States before, during and after World War II will be reviewed to show how important government financing through Reconstruction Finance Corporation loans, construction of facilities by Defense Plant Corporation (a subsidiary of RFC) and 'accelerated amortization' were in the industry's rapid growth. These will be discussed in relationship to the firms that now make up the aluminum industry in the United States.

For many years, the Aluminum Company of America meant the industry in North America. A few attempts to enter the game were made but somehow they always wound up under that one name. These included the Southern Aluminum Company organized by French interests in 1912, and the Quebec Aluminum Company in which J. B. Duke of the tobacco company family joined with a British financier and the president of an Aluminum Die Casting Company.*

A little later, another tobacco heir came into the business, this time through the foil used to package cigarettes. He was

---

*M. J. Peck, *Competition in the Aluminum Industry* Harvard University Press, (1961), p. 8.

R. S. Reynolds and his aluminum foil and Reynolds Metals Company still survive. Duke and his partners traded their interest for American Aluminum shares. In 1939, Reynolds suggested to Senator Lister Hill (Alabama) that the capacity of the aluminum industry should be doubled to meet national security requirements for aircraft. The RFC loaned his company $16 million to build the Lister Hill facility. After Pearl Harbor, the RFC again loaned Reynolds Metals $36 million, this time to build another reduction plant and a sheet mill. In addition to these, the company also operated some of Defense Plant Corporation aluminum facilities.

Another RFC supported entrant into the business was Henry J. Kaiser of shipbuilding fame (also RFC financed). As *Fortune* magazine described Kaiser's and Reynold's entry into aluminum, ordinary men would not have had the aggressiveness to take on as formidable a competitor as Aluminum Company of America. In *Fortune's* words, 'It is possible mere managers might not have had the will and daring to buck Alcoa.' However, we must not lose sight of their RFC as well as other kinds of government support.

With this post-World War II breaking of the barrier, it seemed only natural that another war should see the government again helping would-be aluminum producers. Korea did. This time the major incentive was accelerated amortization* which permitted the write-off of the investment in the short period of five years. This was available not only during the years of conflict but also until the Office of Demobilization called it off on 22 September 1955.

Before the book was closed, Anaconda, Harvey Aluminum and Ormet were in the game. Later, more new producers announced plans: Howmet Corporation, National-Southwire Aluminum, Canada's Noranda Mines, Limited, Revere Copper and Brass, and Amax each bought sites and began building facilities to be completed in the 1970s.

Summary

The world's second most important metal is, for all practical purposes, a twentieth century development. Although it is now based on bauxite, there are many other aluminous materials from which it is or is likely to be produced in the future. There is not now or ever likely to be a shortage of aluminum that

---

*Also available during World War II, but because of private industry's concern about over-expansion, they then preferred the Defense Plant Corporation route.

has expanded to today's 15,000,000 tons from the 7,300 tons turned out in the first year of this century.

As we look at the commercial, industrial and technological development of this one natural resource, it is clear that when government is willing to push, prod and pull an industry, there are no limits on what man can be expected to accomplish.

8. Timber

BY J. W. NOAH AND W. E. DEPUY, JR

Timber, harvested from the world's forest lands, has been woven into the fabric of almost every society on earth. This has been true from the time of man's emergence from the trees, and will continue into the foreseeable and even distant future. It has always had, and will continue to have, myriad applications in man's daily business of feeding, clothing, and sheltering himself.

However, now we hear talk of world timber shortages, of scarcity. To what degree is this true, and to what degree is it not? This brief examination of the world's timber resources is an effort to inform and possibly enlighten those of us concerned with the world's scarce resources.

For highly industrialized and developing agrarian societies alike, timber is a vital resource. The obvious firewood, building materials, toothpicks, telephone poles come easily to mind, but wood and wood derivatives' presence in automobile engine oil filters, satellite communications equipment, and electric cables, do not. As technology expands, man's ability to extract more and more from his timber resources will also grow.

So what is the problem? Is it timber shortage or scarcity? Are we actually running out of wood or are we merely experiencing the same kinds of difficulty in managing timber as we have had in managing other world resources?

To begin with, it was not until the latter part of the nineteenth century in Europe that a new image of forests and timber emerged. Up until this time no one paid much attention to trees. They always seemed to be there when needed, and in sufficient numbers to delay the question: 'what happens if we run out?' The new image of forests, which emerged at this time in certain royal circles, was that they were, in essence, a crop. They needed to be managed, harvested, replanted, and groomed. Forests became royal preserves, and permission was needed to remove so much as a twig. Peasants were allowed to come into the forests and remove the deadwood to fuel their fires, careful thinning of the trees provided ample wood to build homes, and huntsmen trekked the length and breadth of the forests to insure that none violated these royal preserves.

What has Happened?

Using the United States as an example, in the early twentieth century she began to enact legislation which would protect and conserve her timber resources. In a fairly short period of time forestlands, which generally had been thought of as an ubiquitous and inexhaustible commodity, were beginning now to be thought of as national resources, needy of protection, conservation, and to some degree, management. But, with increased demand for wood and wood products, problems surfaced in maintaining the supply of available timber.

America has already experienced temporary shortages of some wood products. Take, for example, the toilet tissue and other paper-related shortages of 1974 when panicky consumers bought and hoarded these products diminishing normal inventories in many urban wholesale and retail outlets. While this type of scarcity created only a transitory discomfort, in the future we could face far more profound disruptions to our life style.

For instance, what validity is there to the ominous predictions concerning residential housing in the United States? Do potential future shortages of building materials, coupled with parallel price increases and skyrocketing costs of land and money, threaten to make this the last generation of American home owners?

One fundamental reason for past wood product shortages and possible shortages in the future is a basic lack of public knowledge on the subject of timber. The wood products industry readily admits that people just do not know much about trees: the growing, harvesting, processing, and converting to other products, as well as reforesting. Consequently, a good many of us are misinformed about the most basic facts concerning timber, such as where the forest grows, how big it is, who runs it, and its impact in this age of concrete and steel, of glass and plastics.

Consider, for example, the location of forestland. How many persons in the United States erroneously think the American forest is out west somewhere? Or, who would surmise that 60 per cent of all commercial forestland in the United States is owned, not by government or industry, but by individual citizens? And how many of us are aware of the scientific progress being made in the creation of 'test tube' trees?

These are just a few of the significant questions to be considered in an examination of the importance of timber's role in this 'world of scarcities'.

The Information Gap

Many people imagine wood to be slightly old-fashioned. It is assumed that the increased technology of our age has made wood an anachronism, replaced by more durable, stronger, resilient materials and yet, wood fibre, wood cellulose, and wood chemicals are vital elements in a bewildering array of modern products that look no more like trees than this book. While most persons may readily associate such every day products as newspapers, books, magazines, and grocery sacks with woodpulp, how many immediately recognize wood's presence in such diverse products as perfumes, ice cream, pills, and artificial blood plasma. Literally hundreds of products that we need, use, or want every day are based on wood and its derivatives.

Perhaps the archaic attitudes towards wood can be traced to its ages-old usage in construction. While Americans still use nearly 5 billion cubic feet of wood a year for new housing, that is actually only about one-third of the total amount of wood they require for modern living.

Surprisingly, an equally large volume of wood is used each year in combination with other substances to produce plastics, explosives, paper items, rayon and other modern chemical products. The remaining third of America's annual timber yield is normally consumed in the production of such cradle-to-grave wooden necessities as cradles and coffins, toys, telephone poles, furniture, fuel and the like.

Wood has clearly become a primary building block of civilization. Naturally, those active in the wood products industry are increasingly concerned about the forest resource information gap. They foresee a potentially severe wood shortage before the year 2000 if we do not act now to prevent it.

Forecasts indicate we will need twice as much wood in 1998 as we needed last year. Can we grow timber fast enough to meet these increasing demands?

Some Partial Solutions

A partial answer to future timber needs lies with small wood-lot owners. The United States Forest Service states that with proper management the yield from its four million private timber stands could be doubled. Such an increase would not solve the problems, but those lots become quite significant when we realize that they contain 41 per cent of the nation's total timber supply.

Also, the growing need for timber resources could be met in part by greater use of wood substitutes. Sometimes, in fact, industry finds substitutes of steel, aluminum, plastics, and glass even more effective. Often, however, these substitutes are far more costly and their substitution creates a plethora of new problems.

As an example, the production of substitutes may mean higher overall demands for energy. Increased pollution may result. In addition, most of the substitutes for wood are derived from non-renewable resources, thus resulting in accelerated depletion of even scarcer raw materials. In this connection, it is important to remember that forestlands can always be reseeded with relatively fast-growing new timber but the raw materials used in wood substitutes may be irreplaceable.

Another possible solution for a country like the United States would appear to be timber imports. As we shall see, however, these are limited by rapidly rising demands for timber throughout the world.

All of these possibilities combined would probably not solve the problems raised by rapidly escalating timber needs. But for the United States there is a solution.

The Emotional Split

There are those who believe too much forest land has already been cleared. Others think forests have been improperly re-planted. Still others look at the pristine wilderness of the forest and ask: Why technology? They see it only as a threat.

Thus we have a fundamental split over forest use. Should forests be maintained as living wilderness museums? As play-grounds for city folk? Or as powerful wood-producing factories consistently turning out endless tons of trees for more homes, toys, paper, exports, jobs, and profits?

This split in attitudes entails an emotional problem . . . simply put: people like trees while foresters and forest product producers like cutting them down. Fortunately for all concerned, however, this emotional split has become a blessing in disguise.

As emotions have led to environmental and economic threats, so these threats have, in turn, led to well-publicized lawsuits. Along the way, lumber and land prices have climbed, thus attract-ing even more attention to timber problems. Out of these seemingly adverse circumstances, a renewed respect for timberlands has evolved, coupled with a greater awareness of the need for forestry renewal, for more efficiency, for better management. Herein may lie America's answer to its growing timber scarcity.

Who Owns the Forests?

When Columbus landed in North America there were about 1 billion acres of forest in this new world. Surprisingly, after almost 500 years of building, paving, burning, exporting, and wasting, 75 per cent of that land is still tree-covered. Moreover, about 50 per cent is still available for commercial use.

Where are the American forests located? Not, as most people think, in the western part of the country. Rather, more than 60 per cent of the continental American forest is located east of the Mississippi. New York, the second most populous state, is 57 per cent forest land. Georgia has more forestland than Colorado—about 3 million acres more. And even New Jersey, one of the most densely populated states, is more than half covered with forest land.

Ownership of these vast timber resources rests primarily in the hands of private individuals. Collectively, they own about 60 per cent of all the nation's commercial forest land, mostly in blocks of seventy acres or less. While many of these small land owners are farmers, an increasing number are absentee landlords who have purchased rural property for investment, recreation, or retirement.

After individuals, the next largest forest landlord is government: state, federal and local governments control about 28 per cent of commercial forests with federal government having by far the largest share. Industry comes in last, owning only 13 per cent.

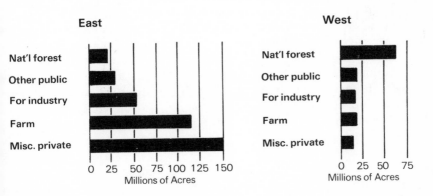

Figure 8.1 Ownership of Commercial Forest Land in the United States by Ownership Category, 1970. Source: *Timber—The Renewable Material*, prepared for the National Commission on Materials Policy, August 1973, pp. 2–14.

With its vastness and varied climate zones, the United States has a unique global position in timber. It grows more than 100 marketable tree species and has enough forestland to cover every inch of Belgium, Great Britain, Denmark, Portugal, The Netherlands, Italy, France, Spain, Japan, Jordan and both Germanies, with enough trees left over to blanket all of Algeria, Austria, and Israel.

A Woodland Revolution

There are well-defined hints that America's timberlands are already undergoing a major technological and scientific revolution, a revolution that is radically changing the face of its vast woodlands.

Chemists, for example, are on the verge of creating 'test-tube' trees derived from the cells of another tree. Other scientists are scouring the woods for seeds and branch cuttings to cross-breed 'super trees'. These would be magnificent, fast-growing specimens bred specifically for commercial attributes, much like the hybrid corns that revolutionized farming half a century ago. Meanwhile, sawmill operators, using radically thinner saw blades to maximize the yield of each log, study computerized television monitors that automatically diagram the best cut. Overhead, helicopter pilots scatter tons of artificially-colored tree seeds to fool hungry birds. Huge machines roam the forests, snipping entire trees off at ground level, then passing them through pulpers that consume 40-foot logs in nine seconds. Entire forests are fertilized and thinned with relative ease, thus producing harvestable growth decades earlier than nature can.

Such miraculous developments at a time of growing concern over the world's ability to meet future demands, hold tremendous future significance for the consumers, their woodlands, their housing, the economy, the balance of payments and land use.

Industrial forestry has proven that such technology, coupled with intensive management, can greatly increase wood growth. Intensive management is part of the reason that industrial forestland today produces 62 per cent more wood per acre than government acreage and 42 per cent more than individually-owned parcels.

These industrial practices would be familiar in theory to any tree farmer: rapid regeneration of the forest to keep the land in production; use of the best available seed stock; careful spacing of the growing crop to assure optimum sunlight, moisture, and soil nutrients; and fertilization to encourage rapid growth.

Professional foresters say that America's forests, if managed intensively, can meet the challenge of the future – that the country can produce enough wood to meet a doubling in demand. The stakes are high.

A Global View

The timber situation in the United States has been used to develop some important issues for policy debate on the predicted timber scarcity. Before analyzing the demand/supply relationships for timber, we shall note the world's timber resources. Forests cover about 28 per cent of the world's land area, or about 9 billion of the 32 billion acres of land on our globe.

Although estimates vary widely, the Food and Agriculture Organization of the United Nations (FAO) believes about 60 per cent of this forested land area may be suitable and available for timber harvesting. The remaining 40 per cent comprises lands reserved for parks, nature preserves, watershed protection, non-productive forestlands, and other non-timber uses.

As indicated by the data in Table 8.1, about one-third of the forested land supports softwoods and two-thirds hardwoods. Most of the softwood acreage, more than 1,300 million acres, is in the Soviet Union, followed closely by North America with almost 1,100 million acres. All the rest of the world combined claims only 425 million acres of softwoods and about half of that is in Europe.

Latin America has the world's largest timber reserves, preponderantly hardwood. In fact, Latin America boasts slightly more than half of the estimated hardwood growing stock in the entire world. Africa, as well as East and South-east Asia, has large volumes of hardwoods.

The total volume of growing stock is only one factor determining a country's importance as a source of timber supply. Institutional or political constraints, physical accessability, species and quality of timber, and availability of capital for development have profound effects on volumes of timber harvested. Latin America, as an example, has about one-third of the world's wood reserves but harvested less than 4 per cent of the world's industrial wood supply during the period 1967–9. The region as a whole is a net importer of wood products.

With this general background on world timber supply, we shall consider the hardwood and softwood situations in more detail. As shown in the accompanying tables, supplies of hardwood and softwood vary drastically in most areas and thus must be clearly separated.

As for hardwood, Latin American and African forests rank

Table 8.1 Land and Forest Areas in the World (Million acres)

Area	1950–2			1967–9		
	Total	Softwoods	Hardwoods	Total	Softwoods	Hardwoods
North America	11,017	8,933	2,083	14,548	11,864	2,684
Latin America	1,095	424	671	1,554	706	847
Europe	6,391	5,191	1,201	8,616	6,179	2,436
Africa	530	35	494	1,201	177	1,024
Asia (except Japan and USSR)	1,942	742	1,201	3,778	1,130	2,648
Japan	953	847	106	1,730	1,095	636
USSR	6,250	5,402	847	10,205	9,039	1,165
Pacific Area	388	106	282	636	318	318
WORLD	28,566	21,680	6,885	42,266	30,508	11,758

Source: Food and Agriculture Organization of the United Nations, *Supply of Wood Materials for Housing*, World Consultation on the Use of Wood in Housing, Secretariat Paper, Section 2, 1971

number one and number two, respectively, in size. Asia, excluding Japan and the Soviet Union, has one-sixth of the world's available hardwood forestland. The remaining hardwood forest (25 per cent) is divided among Europe, Japan, the Soviet Union, and the Pacific Area.

With only 8 per cent of the world's hardwood growing stock, North America cuts almost 23 per cent of the industrial hardwood. Europe produces nearly as much from less than one-fourth as much growing stock. Asia, excluding Japan and the Soviet Union, has nearly twice as much hardwood growing stock as North America but production is about the same as that produced in North America. Growth in production of hardwood has been most rapid in Asia and Africa where both have more than doubled their output since 1950–2. Latin America, as mentioned above, has over half of the world's hardwood timber, and yet it accounts for less than 10 per cent of production.

Table 8.2 Forest Growing Stock in the World (Billion Cubic Feet)

Area	*Total*	*Softwoods*	*Hardwoods*
North America	2,083	1,395	689
Latin America	4,340	99	4,241
Europe	473	290	184
Africa	1,232	11	1,222
Asia (except Japan and USSR)	1,444	212	1,232
Japan	67	35	32
USSR	2,807	2,345	463
Pacific Area	177	11	166
WORLD	12,623	4,396	8,227

Source: Food and Agriculture Organization of the United Nations. *Supply of Wood Materials for Housing*, World Consultation on the Use of Wood in Housing, Secretariat Paper, Section 2, 1971

Hardwood supply expansion is possible in most of the world's tropical areas, but increases appear most likely to take place in the South-east Asia areas. Most tropical areas with large hardwood supplies face basic problems of infrastructure requirements plus shortage of capital.

Turning to softwood, the Soviet Union, which, as we have seen, has the largest softwood forest available for wood production in the world, also has the largest volume of softwood growing stock. Amounting to more than two billion cubic feet, or about

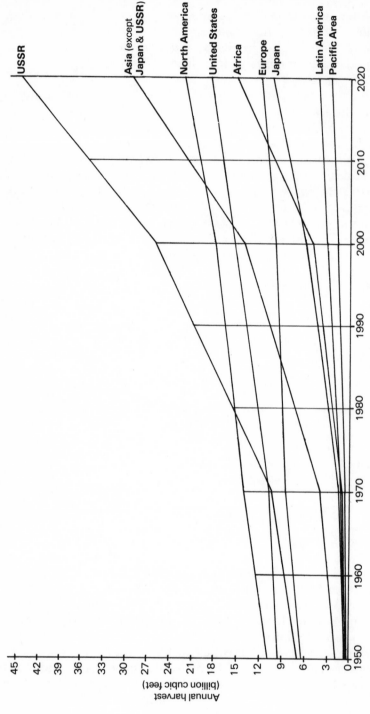

Figure 8.2 Average Annual Harvest of Industrial Roundwood Projected to Year 2020. Sources: (1950–67) United States Department of Agriculture, *The Outlook for Timber in the United States*, Forest Resource Report No. 20, July 1974, p. 134. (1967–2020) Calculations by J. W. Noah based on growth rates evident to 1969

53 per cent of the world total, most of it is in Northern Russia and Siberia. The United States and Canada combined have nearly one-third of the world's softwood growing stock, while Europe has slightly less than 7 per cent.

North America harvests more softwood than any other region, about 40 per cent of the world's total. Ninety per cent of the softwoods cut for industrial use are produced in North America, the Soviet Union and Europe. Expansion of softwood production has been most rapid in recent years in the Soviet Union where the greatest area and volume of unexploited softwood forests lie.

Prospects for significant additions to softwood timber exports appear to be limited to Canada and the Soviet Union. Both of these countries are characterized by having most of their timber resources under government control, and both have indicated a desire to develop areas where timber has gone virtually unexploited. Government policies as well as trends in prices and markets will be significant in determining how rapidly expansion of their timber industry takes place.

It is with the above hardwood-softwood supply figures fixed in mind that we turn to Figure 8.2 for a graphic portrayal of the trend in world timber harvests. As we study this graph, it is interesting to recall the Sixth World Forestry Congress which was convened by the FAO in Madrid. The 1966 meeting was attended by 2,800 foresters from ninety-one countries. A FAO forecast at the time predicted that demand for primary forest products, especially from underdeveloped nations, would double within the coming fifteen years. FAO officials suggested that future supplies could be assured if 370 million acres of new, man-made forests were developed in Latin America and Africa.

At the time of writing, the rate of growth in annual average harvest of industrial roundwood in Africa is responding to the FAO suggestion. Latin America's rate of increase as indicated in Figure 8.2 is not.

The principal factors determining future world consumption of timber are population and economic growth on the demand side, and production of timber resources and cost of processing, transportation and marketing on the supply side. Demographers have predicted that the world's population will top 6 billion people by the year 2000, about double the 1960 population. Expected increases in population and economic growth, especially in the developed countries, suggest a large increase in demand for wood products.

According to the FAO's Provisional Indicative World Plan for Agricultural Development (IWP), world prospects for production, consumption, and trade in forest products in 1975 and 1985 is fairly well defined. Their main conclusions regarding demand are:

> The demand for processed forest products is continuing to rise at rates which will take world consumption of sawnwood in 1985 to more than 40 per cent above the 1962 level; of wood-based panels to 260 per cent higher, and of pulp and paper to over 240 per cent higher.
>
> Consumption will grow in developing countries at much faster rates than the world average, as income elasticity of demand for most processed forest products is higher at low income levels than at high ones. Consumption of sawnwood will be almost 150 per cent above consumption in 1962, whereas demands for the various types of wood-based panels and grades of paper and paper board will increase by four to ten times the 1962 level.
>
> Despite the rising proportion of world consumption that will be accounted for by developing countries, over 90 per cent of the world's aggregate consumption of processed forest products will take place in developed countries by 1985.
>
> World consumption of unprocessed forest products such as wood used directly in the round and fuelwood will not increase significantly. This will be the result of the continuing decline in consumption in developed countries counterbalanced by a relatively slow rate of increase in the less developed parts of the world.

One of the most significant aspects of developments in the 1950s and 1960s was that Europe, the United States, and Japan accounted for 60 per cent of the world's industrial wood use. All three areas are heavily dependent on timber from other countries and will be competing for wood on the world market in the years ahead.

Timber Demand/Supply Relationships in the United States

National consumption of industrial roundwood, i.e., all timber removed from the forest except fuelwood, is expected to rise from a 1960 level of 11.5 million cubic feet to 18.7 billion cubic feet in 1980, according to an estimate from Resources For The Future. Extrapolating that estimate to the year 2000, the non-profit organization predicted consumption by the end of this century would reach more than 32 billion cubic feet. Particularly significant, and alarming, is the fact that the study saw no hope for a parallel increase in commercial forestland area. While present US Forest Service predictions are more encouraging, the question remains: 'will the United States be prepared to provide the supply for its demands projected for the year 2000?'

Demands on American forests for softwood timber products, after allowance for imports and exports, have been projected to increase from 8.8 billion cubic feet in 1970 to a range of 11.1 to 15.1 billion cubic feet by the year 2000. The range predicted by the Forest Service is based on specified price assumptions and a medium level projection of population and economic growth.

Comparisons of their supply and demand projections for softwoods indicate that under the economic and other conditions assumed in their analysis, fairly substantial increases in prices of timber products relative to the general price level will be necessary to balance demands and available supplies of timber.

In the same way, demand for hardwood timber products after import/export allowances is estimated by the Forest Service to rise from about 2.9 billion cubic feet in 1970 to a range of 5.3–6.8 billion cubic feet by the year 2000. The range is estimated under alternative price assumptions and a medium level of population and economic growth. Potentially available supplies of hardwood timber from American forests may increase from 2.9 billion cubic feet in 1970 to about 7.4 billion cubic feet by the year 2000. Thus, total supplies of hardwood potentially available in terms of cubic feet exceed projected demands throughout the period from now through to the end of the century. This implies that increases in relative prices are not likely. Wide differences in timber quality and availability, however, indicate a variable outlook for supply-price relationships.

Anticipated increases in timber prices and aggravated supply problems will have significant impacts on the softwood lumber and plywood industries. Prospective limitations of timber supplies and increases in prices will limit expansion potentials for these products' use in housing and other markets. Correspondingly, greater dependence will probably be placed on competitive materials for many of the same uses.

In an effort to augment the supply for the current demand for timber in the United States, the Department of Agriculture has released 10.8 billion board feet of timber from its national forests for sale in 1976. Furthermore, in an attempt to establish a hedge against future expected increases in demand, the Forest Service has been directed to stockpile an inventory of 2 billion board feet prepared for sale by the end of 1976. These sorts of governmental actions come from the realization that for the United States, not only private forest related industries, but the government as well, must actively participate in the intensive management of this vital resource.

Long-range estimates of American timber demand and supply include significant volumes of both imports and exports of wood products. The Forest Service estimates that net imports will increase from 8 per cent of American consumption in 1970 to about 15 per cent of projected demands in the year 2000.

The potential for substantial increases in net imports of timber products appears to be limited by physical availability of timber supplies from other countries and by economic and political factors. Greater dependence on net imports would, of course, increase the country's need for foreign exchange and result in adverse impacts on the American balance of payments position.

Summary

Looking at Figure 8.2 there is ample reason to believe that the United States is losing its position as the Saudia Arabia of the timber world. Increasing America's net imports will, of course, drive relative prices up, and because timber is likely to remain one of the country's most important raw materials, it is imperative that something be done to improve the Nation's average annual harvest of industrial roundwood.

During the decades of the 1950s and the 1960s the United States growth in annual timber harvested increased by 1 per cent per year. The Soviet Union on the other hand demonstrated a growth in annual harvest of almost 3 per cent per year. Extrapolating these growth rates indicates clearly that the Soviet Union has caught up and perhaps surpassed the United States in harvesting industrial roundwood. Moreover, the Russians will be harvesting about 70 per cent more timber than the United States by the year 2000. Projecting growth rates to the year 2020, the United States is shown in a poor third position in timber harvest unless something is done to change her rate of growth.

Fortunately, there are opportunities for intensified timber management and utilization in the United States. Measures to increase timber growth and harvest, however, will require substantial public and private investments. Large expenditures also will be needed to provide the plants and equipment necessary to extend timber supply via improved utilization in the harvest processing, and use of timber products.

Potential imbalances between rising demands for timber and available supplies are part of the world-wide problem of assuring adequate raw materials for housing and a multitude of other uses and products. A shift from timber to a greater dependence on substitute materials may be possible, but it would entail problems of cost, pollution, dependence on foreign suppliers, and additional balance of payments problems. Increasing timber supplies from domestic forests, while assuring a balance with other uses and environmental protection, is an alternative that is technically and economically feasible even though time and substantial expenditures will be necessary. The outlook for timber in the United States is thus a matter of serious and far-reaching public and private concern.

Although the growth of all wood products combined is less than spectacular, its projection will entail a considerably expanded drain on wood supply. In some areas of the world, Japan, Western Europe, and the United States, increasing levels of imports will be necessary to meet their growing demands. Although much of the additional supply may well come from Canada and the Soviet Union, demands on tropical areas will probably increase substantially. There will be opportunities for increased investment in plantations in areas where rapid growth can be obtained.

We have seen that the Soviet Union has a far greater forest area, mostly softwoods, than Europe and North America combined. With about a third of the world's forest land, the USSR provides about 20 per cent of the world's timber cut, less than that in the United States and presumably well below the level that could be sustained. The Soviet Union is now exporting softwood logs to Japan and lumber to Europe. The extent to which exports increase, and how fast, will depend on their success in handling the problems involved in extending the forest industry into the remote regions as well as that of meeting growing domestic demands.

It is generally expected that in most areas of the world the increasing demand and limited supply will lead to price increases. However, the extent to which this may result in substitution of wood by other materials is a matter of conjecture, and closely tied to the relationship in prices between timber products and their alternatives.

9. Zinc

BY KURT BLEICKEN

Zinc is mined in significant quantities on all continents. Five countries: Canada, Mexico, Australia, Peru, and Japan mine 60 per cent of the non-communist world supply. The United States alone produces 10 per cent of that part of the supply. Among the communist producers, the Soviet Union is the largest source of zinc with a mining output considerably larger than that of the United States. Total world and American identified and probable reserves are shown in Table 9.1.

Table 9.1 Identified and Undiscovered Zinc Resources of the World and the United States (Millions of Tons)

	Identified Resources	Undiscovered Resources	Total
TOTAL WORLD			
Recoverable	235	345	580
Sub-economic	1,275	3,230	4,505
TOTAL	1,510	3,575	5,085
UNITED STATES			
Recoverable	45	60	105
Sub-economic	75	230	305
TOTAL	120	290	410
REST OF WORLD			
Recoverable	190	285	475
Sub-economic	1,200	3,000	4,200
TOTAL	1,390	3,285	4,675

Source: United States Minerals Resources, Geological Survey Professional Paper 820, Washington DC 1973, p. 706

Zinc Consumption in the United States

Probably the most interesting thing about zinc in the United States is the case developed later in this chapter for little or no growth in consumption of the metal from now through the year 2000. This has profound implications for both the producer nations as well as for the American and world zinc industry. But first, what is this material and what is it used for?

Zinc represents a marked contrast to aluminum in many ways. Aluminum, the 'wunderkind' metal, is easily identified both visually and statistically as to its end use. Everyone recognizes an aluminum frying pan, aluminum wire, or aluminum siding on a house. Very few people recognize a brass door knocker as one with a crucial zinc content, or that certain paints because of the hidden identity problem contain zinc oxide, or that a galvanized bucket is zinc coated steel.

Statistically it is virtually impossible to follow zinc through to its final use. The best we can do is to describe the intermediate consumption of zinc and make an intelligent guess as to where it ends up, as shown in Table 9.2.

Table 9.2 Uses of Zinc (Millions of Tons)

	1960	1971
Galvanizing	0.3	0.48
Brass Products	0.1	0.15
Die Casting	0.3	0.50
Oxides	0.1	0.04
Other	0.1	0.08
TOTAL	0.9	1.25

Source: United States Bureau of Mines, *Minerals Yearbook*, 1970 and 1971

Galvanizing or coating steel with zinc protects it from rusting and also helps electrical corrosion. Most of the galvanized steel ends up in the construction industry and thus is tied to the growth of that industry. Die-casting, or the making of molds for casting other materials, was the most important consumer of zinc in 1971. Copper when alloyed with zinc produces brass. That product is corrosion resistant, much stronger and more machinable than copper. Zinc oxide, the smallest of the identifiable uses, ends up in paints, pharmaceuticals, cosmetics and a broad range of other products.

The history of total zinc consumption and the patterns of zinc consumption *per capita* in the United States are shown in Table 9.3.

Table 9.3 Consumption of Zinc *Per Capita*, United States

	US Zinc Consumption (*1,000* tons)	US Population (*millions*)	Pounds of Zinc Per Capita
1900	103	76	2.71
1905	199	84	4.74
1910	266	92	5.78
1915	358	100	7.16
1920	361	106	6.8
1925	496	116	8.6
1930	493	123	8.0
1935	423	127	6.7
1940	606	132	9.2
1945	853	133	12.8
1950	985	152	13.0
1955	1,140	165	13.8
1960	1,159	180	12.9
1965	1,354	194	13.9
1970	1,187	204	11.6
1971	1,254	207	12.1
1972	1,418	208	13.6
1973	1,520	209	14.5

Source: United States Bureau of Mines, *Minerals Yearbook*

As is evident, zinc usage grew at a rapid rate from 1900–45 with the only major dip occurring in the great depression. In 1945 consumption *per capita* began to level off. Since then the figures have stayed in a very narrow range, 12–14 pounds, for almost thirty years. This has occurred in a period when *per capita* consumption of materials of all kinds was rising very rapidly in America. The reason for this relatively bad performance is that zinc was one of the metals most easily replaced by new materials that were coming along. Plastic buckets and trash cans have made almost obsolete their old galvanized predecessors. The new plastic replacements are lighter, cheaper to produce, quieter in use, dentproof and practically indestructible. The use of zinc in brass has been slowed by its relatively high price and by the introduction of substitutes. Anodized aluminum as well as plastics have filled a demand for a cheaper, even though sometimes aesthetically less attractive, material.

Demand in the Future

To belabor the obvious, the growth of any metals industry such as zinc, with a stable usage *per capita*, depends solely on an increase in the population. We shall take a look at one past projection of zinc consumption made in 1963 by Resources for the Future, Incorporated, as well as more recent estimates prepared by the National Commission on Materials Policy in 1973.

The 1963 Resources for the Future calculations were based on the best population projections then available. Their low estimate of 1.7 million tons of zinc to be consumed by the United States in the year 2000 was made on the basis of a population forecast of 280 million people, which implies a *per capita* consumption of 12.1 pounds. The middle and higher calculations by RFF used population estimates of about 320 million and 440 million Americans respectively. These can now be dismissed as unlikely in view of the current population experience.

The 1973 estimates of the National Commission on Materials Policy of 3.2 million short tons of zinc to be used into the year 2000 are more difficult to understand. Using their mid-range population forecast for the year 2000–275 million people–their consumption figure would indicate a jump in *per capita* use from the current 12–14 pound range to over 23 pounds per person. Since *per capita* zinc usage has remained constant for the last thirty years, this dramatic rise should be explained somewhere in the Commission's report, but is not.

The United States Bureau of Mines 1974 Commodity Data Summaries, has this to say:

> Demand for zinc covers a wide range of industrial applications and while aluminum, plastics, and improved steels pose threats to some of these markets, it seems likely that inroads by substitute materials will be offset by advances in zinc application technology which will maintain the upward trend in total demand.

It would seem more logical to use zinc *per capita* assumptions based on two different premises. First, the assumption that usage *per capita* remains constant over the next twenty-five years. Second, that the usage per person declines over the next twenty-five years. In order to calculate a high-low estimate, the lower zinc *per capita* assumption will be multiplied by the lower population series, and the higher zinc *per capita* assumption by the higher of the two United States Census Bureau series which we regard as reasonable.

Table 9.4

	US Dept of Census Series E Population (millions of people)	×	Per Capita Zinc Consumption (pounds)	=	Projected Total Zinc Required (1,000 tons)
1970	205		11.6		1,180
1980	224		13.0		1,460
1990	247		13.0		1,600
2000	264		13.0		1,700
	Series F Population		Per Capita		
1970	205		11.6		1,180
1980	222		11.0		1,220
1990	239		10.0		1,190
2000	251		9.0		1,130

The first series of estimates produces exactly what the 1963 Resources for the Future Study calculated in their low projections for the year 2000. The second series shows little or no change in zinc usage through the year 2000. These estimates are compared in Figure 9.1.

The first assumption, that *per capita* usage will remain fairly constant can be justified by several arguments. First, thirty years of level consumption would not suggest an increasing usage over the proximate future. Second, while there is a continued substitution of other materials for zinc, there is also the possibility that some new applications for zinc may appear to offset that trend. Third, the probability of no step-function improvement in the standard of living over the next quarter century would argue against any broad increase in total level of this material's usage in the United States.

The second assumption, that American zinc consumption *per capita* will decline over the next twenty-five years can be even more strongly argued. A decline in the total materials and energy consumed appears likely because of the sharp increase in energy prices and likely increasing prices for many of the natural resource materials. Then there is the possibility that aluminum, plastics, and other new materials will continue to be substituted for zinc on an expanding list of uses.

Finally, as the American population growth slows down and begins to stabilize toward the end of the century, that portion of the growth in the economy which is dependent on an expanding population will be missing. Population pressure that is highly materials-oriented will decline. New highways with galvanized

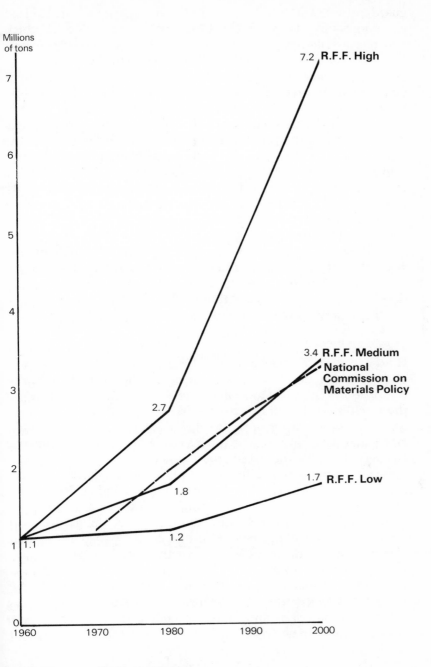

Figure 9.1   Projections of Zinc Consumption. Source: *Resources in America's Future*, Johns Hopkins University Press, 1963; *Material Needs and the Environment Today and Tomorrow*, 1973

guard rails, new housing and/or new office space with galvanized
air conditioning ductwork are illustrative of the industries which
will feel a slackening in demand as population pressure eases.
It is quite obvious that with slow or no growth in the American
population these industries and others will tend more towards
being repair and replacement users of zinc products. By 2030–50
when the United States is likely to attain a population plateau,
the fortunes of many industries will depend solely on increases
or decreases in personal consumption standards because the
nation will require a relatively stable quantity of highway systems,
transportation systems, housing and office space infrastructures.
It is clear that in this extreme case the nation will no longer
require 42,500 pounds * of all materials per person, per year
as the United States did in 1972.

To see what would happen with a slow decline, a dip from
11 pounds *per capita* per year to 9 pounds *per capita* by the
year 2000, we made some calculations. The result was a stable
level of usage throughout the period. If one assumes a further
decline in *per capita* consumption, the industry would operate
at considerably lower levels than it does today.

Future Possibilities

If we can make a reasonable case for a leveling off in the growth
of demand for zinc or even a downward trend in total consumption in the United States, what implications does this have for
the world's producers of this material? America currently consumes about a quarter of the world's output of zinc, which indicates that anything that happens to American demand will
strongly influence the world zinc market.

But perhaps there is a further implication. We have suggested
earlier in the chapter that perhaps zinc is used widely in the
building of the American economic infrastructure. In other
words, that most zinc goes into those physical things necessary
for housing, schooling, communications and transportation, for
instance. When the population growth slows and at the point
when it comes to a zero rate, what happens to the infrastructure?
It is naive to assume that all growth of the infrastructure will
stop, but there certainly will be a marked decline in the amount
of money, materials, and labor expended on these systems as
we shift from a new construction phase to a repair and replacement mode.

---

*National Commission on Materials Policy, 1973.

Closer study of the economics of zinc reveals some interesting differences between this metal and others, such as aluminum. The price of aluminum will largely determine whether wood or aluminum is used in the housing industry. In contrast, within fairly broad limits, the demand for zinc has very little to do with its price. In other words, zinc demand is price inelastic. Since only a small bit of zinc is required to make an expensive brass product, it really does not matter whether the zinc costs 10 cents a pound or 30 cents. Conversely, if the price of zinc plummeted from 20 cents a pound to a nickel, it would hardly be an inducement to buy more. In most applications the cost of the zinc content, in relation to the price of the end product, is very small indeed. Therefore, the price of the metal can go up or down, while the industrial system consumes what it needs.

Just as inelastic as is its demand, is the supply situation. It takes a great deal of time and promise of high return on investment to open up a new zinc mine. *Resources in America's Future* described how the United States subsidized the industry in an effort to stimulate domestic zinc production during both World War II and the Korean War, and noted the lack of success these efforts enjoyed. The problem probably lies in lead-time. It takes five years and perhaps as long as seven years to open a new zinc mine and get it running smoothly. Then once it is opened it becomes very important to keep it operating on a continuous basis.

There is a great capital cost involved in opening a mine, and if it is shut down it suddenly becomes a very large and embarrassing non-productive capital asset sitting on someone's balance sheet. If the mine-owner happens to be a small country, other pressures to keep operating emerge. It may be more important to have the mine open and people working than to have a balanced national budget.

If we assume that demand for zinc grows until a shortage develops, because the consuming companies have to have the zinc for their end products, and because the price of zinc in those products is a very small component of the end product price, the companies will bid more for the zinc. Zinc buyers, seeing a shortage developing, tend to buy for inventory, thus increasing apparent demand. As a result, the price may double in a few years. A mining company, seeing increased demand and higher prices starts to open up a new mine. Five to seven years later it may be in production. Then they discover that one or more competitive mines were also opened and are now producing, too. More production probably means the price will go down as fast as it went up, since many producers would rather cut prices than restrict production.

Running alongside the classical supply and demand patterns of the mining industry are the political effects of changing attitudes of the people and the governments about mining.

In the late 1950s in the United States, mineral prices had fallen for a number of reasons, including the 1958 recession. The American zinc mining industry was in trouble. Demand was down, prices were down and unemployment was up sharply. The government put quotas on foreign imports of zinc. The domestic price rose above the world price and, in the next three years, domestic production moved up about 30 per cent. So did the price of the metal.

In the 1950s the United States government thought it correct to protect one of our basic metals industries at the expense of the American consumer. Now, fifteen years later, we are facing a very similar set of conditions. Again, the zinc industry is in trouble. Each year over the past five years domestic mine production has gone down. Mines and smelters are closing at a very rapid rate. The country is using more zinc each year but this is coming from imports of slab zinc.

This time it appea s that the United States government is inadvertantly helping to put its industry out of business. New pollution control standards, new rules governing smelter emission standards, new safety regulations, all are rapidly adding to the cost of mining and smelting operations in the United States. We are not arguing the rights or wrongs of the situation, merely that in a very short space of time, something rather basic in the country's attitude towards the zinc industry has changed.

In contrast, foreign, privately owned mines and foreign nationalized mines are currently enjoying looser environmental restrictions. These lower standards, along with less expensive labor, have made the United States product easy prey for foreign competition. Domestic mine production is declining. This is not because of depletion, but rather results of the purchaser's natural tendency to buy zinc at the lowest price.

It is interesting to speculate that increased resources may just be to the advantage of the United States in the long run. While foreign ore is currently being depleted, this country is moderating its consumption of its ore.

Now we come to the critical question. Is zinc likely to be a truly scarce resource in the next twenty-five years?

Using our higher and lower projections of zinc consumption in the year 2000 (1.7 million tons per year, and 1.1 million tons respectively), American cumulative demand for zinc should fall between 30 million and 40 million tons over the next twenty-five years. If the United States were to rely exclusively on its own zinc resources it could quite seriously deplete the identified and recoverable ore bodies during that time period. But this is not the case. The United States is not relying heavily on its resources. Instead it is now producing well under 500,000 tons per year domestically and importing the rest. At this rate, it would use less than 12.5 million tons of domestic zinc, less than one-third of that country's resources.

What about the world supply and demand situation? Assuming that world demand continues to grow at 3 per cent per year over the next twenty-five years (which we suspect is too high), world consumption would increase from 6 million tons per year to about 13 million tons per year, a cumulative total consumption of 240 million tons. This is very close to the current estimates of world reserves, but substantially less than the calculated economically recoverable world zinc resources.

In other words, if the resource estimates are reliable, we have enough zinc in current reserves to just about meet demand to the year 2000.

However, during the next twenty-five years, we can probably count on technological improvements. Improved techniques of finding new zinc deposits will tend to convert undiscovered resources into identified resources. At the same time, the world's zinc companies will probably find ways of economically smelting lower grades of zinc ore than are currently acceptable.

Even using a high rate of growth, zinc resources appear to be adequate. If mine exploration goes well, the world will probably still have adequate reserves in the year 2000. If the world growth of zinc consumption is slower than 3 per cent per year, there will not be a noticeable problem for a long, long time.

10. Copper

BY DAVID NOVICK

Copper reserves and resources in the world are large relative both to current levels of production and consumption and to those anticipated to the end of the century. Production, however, will depend on such factors as the price of copper, the rates at which new copper deposits are discovered, the extent to which identified resources can be and are transferred to reserves, and the construction of additional mining, smelting and refining capacity. Three other problems affect the availability of the material: (i) environmental considerations in both mine production and smelter facilities; (ii) safety and health regulations; (iii) access to additional copper-bearing areas.

The average content of copper in the earth's crust is 58 parts per million, so that theoretically 5×10^{15} tons (50,000,000,000,000,000) tons is there for the taking. The amount of copper available in local concentration and amenable to recovery is vastly less. Even in heavily mineralized areas such as the south-western portion of the United States, the part of the crust known to contain copper at grades above one-tenth of 1 per cent Cu, is no more than one-hundredth of 1 per cent. If the same mineralization factor could be applied to all the world and 10 per cent of the total was accessible, then the copper available would be 150 billion tons. Inasmuch as the south-western United States is one of the most richly mineralized copper regions in the world, the figure just quoted can be postulated as an upper limit for the amount of copper that can be produced by present or future mining methods.

This theoretic figure can be given a more realistic position by using the United States Bureau of Mines *Commodity Data Summaries*, 1975 (Table 10.1).

The world has abundant reserves despite dire forecasts made from time to time. The 1952 Paley report to President Truman predicted that the United States would be out of copper in the

Table 10.1 World Copper Mine Production and Reserves
(Thousands of Short Tons)

	Mine Production 1973	1974	Reserves
United States	1,718	1,588	90,000
Canada	899	900	40,000
Chile	819	910	70,000
Peru	241	240	30,000
Zaire	538	560	20,000
Zambia	779	760	30,000
Other Free World	1,683	1,742	95,000
Communist countries (except Yugoslavia)	1,180	1,240	55,000
WORLD TOTAL	7,857	7,940	430,000

1970s. In 1973 the Club of Rome study expanded on the idea of limited natural resources and predicted a world-wide disaster by the end of the century.

In the real world, future availability will be determined by price, technology and investment requirements. The studies referenced have put too much emphasis on projections of past experience in both demand and supply. We must now have some new projections based on realistic assumptions about changes in methods of producing copper and substitutes for it. Such analyses must go beyond changes in materials and into new ways of transmitting communications and energy rather than the factors usually considered in studies made to date.

Copper and its Uses

All civilizations from pre-historic times to the present have been very dependent on the 'red metal'. The wealth and power of many of the great empires of the past can be attributed in large measure to their possession of the material. In the beginning copper found in its native state was pounded into shape. Later, it was melted and cast. The beginning of the industry, as we know it now, took place centuries ago when it was discovered that copper could be smelted from its ores. In any case there is little doubt that copper and gold were the first metals to be used. Since gold was too soft for weapons and tools, it was copper that served utilitarian purposes.

Its essential value arose from its malleability and ease of working, resistance to corrosion, and of course availability. In many cases it was used because of its attractive colors in both alloyed and unalloyed forms. It is a most versatile material and has a wide range of uses. Historically, the principal ones were tools, cooking utensils and vessels, weapons, pipes and objects of art. The use of copper based on its physical characteristics as well as its capacity for forming numerous alloys has given it a myriad of applications. These range from the fine threads of wire in a transistor radio to the massive bronze screws or propellors on ocean-going vessels.

More than half of all copper produced is used in connection with electricity and it is this application that has made for the spectacular growth in the demand for it over the last fifty years. Copper consumption reached an early peak during World War II. Since then the rate of growth in consumption has slowed down. Much of this is due to substitutes for copper, for example, aluminum and plastics, but, to a lesser extent, is also due to changes in means for performing functions that in the past called for the 'red metal'. Microwave towers for long distance transmission of television programs and telephone messages is one example; communication satellites are another. Changes of this kind are replacing billions of miles of copper wire in overland and underwater cables. There are potential new modes for electric power transmission being studied and if successful, most of them would replace the copper cable and wire now used for moving power from generators to users.

Production, Consumption and Price

Copper is a highly re-cyclable material. Some 65 per cent of all of the material ever produced is still in use. This means that mine production of the ore is particularly price sensitive, which makes for wide market swings with short-term surpluses or shortages having a marked effect on price.

In 1971 and 1972, there was an apparent surplus of copper and prices were lower than in the 1968–70 period. Near the end of 1971 production, under the Allende régime in Chile, started to drop. At about the same time, Zambia encountered transportation problems in moving its production, and pollution regulations started to affect smelter production in the United States.

Demand turned up in late 1972, as the European, Japanese and American economies entered the boom phase. By early 1973 world-wide consumption was increasing at a 9 per cent a year rate. This trend ran into new supply problems in the summer of 1973. Those in Canada and the United States were the major ones, but labor problems in Chile and technical ones in Zambia also cut down supplies. By early 1975 demand had receded and Chilean production had improved significantly. As a result, in the summer of 1975, the price on the London Metals Exchange* stood at 53.36 cents per pound. That was its lowest level in ten years. This was a marked contrast to the $1.52 peak established in April 1974.

The price of copper impacts the material's outlook in several ways. First, it is a major factor in determining the extent to which substitutes like aluminum replace it in many applications; and second, it determines the profitability of producing the material. Profit in turn makes the industry able to attract the capital needed to finance the expansions called for by even moderate rates of growth in *per capita* consumption. We will turn to the investment problem in a moment. Now, let us look at world-wide production and consumption.

As shown in Table 10.2, world-wide mine output and consumption both more than doubled between 1952 and 1972. Of the 4,460,000 ton increase in mine output, it is worth noting that 1,440,000 tons came from Chile, Peru, the Philippines, Zaire and Zambia, all of them unimportant in the consumption picture. Canada contributed a net amount of 444,000 tons since output was up 544,000 tons and use only 99,000.

The greatest expansion was in the USSR but its increased use of copper took practically all of the high level production. The United States was the second highest scorer but its increase was largely offset by a higher use of the material. The biggest jump in copper consumption was in Japan where the figures went from 103,000 tons to 1,046,000. Japan produces only 10 per cent of its requirements. Europe, which consumes about a third of the world's copper, is in much the same position. It mined 280,000 tons and used 2,550,000 in 1972.

So, it is clear that the use of copper around the world follows a different pattern than that of the location of the ore. To improve their trading or bargaining position, Chile, Peru, Zaire and Zambia formed a producers alliance in 1967. So far, CIPEC (based on its French Name, Conseil Intergouvernemental des Pays Exportateurs de Cuivre) has not been an effective cartel. Twice in 1975, it cut back production to hold up prices, but the recession had piled up more than 1 million tons of copper

---

*For a readable discussion of the London Metals Exchange and its operations, see Sir Ronald Prain, *Copper: The Anatomy of an Industry*, Mining Journal Books (London, 1975).

Table 10.2 World Mine and Smelter Production and Consumption of Copper in Selected Countries, 1952 and 1972 (1,000 Short Tons)

Country	PRODUCTION (1952)		CONSUMPTION	PRODUCTION (1972)		CONSUMPTION
	Mine	*Smelter*		*Mine*	*Smelter*	
TOTAL AMERICAS	1,763	1,833	1,637	3,587	3,130	2,395
Brazil	(a)	(a)	22	(a)	(a)	90
Canada	258	223	130	801	510	229
Chile	450	422	(a)	790	695	(a)
Peru[b]	34	23	(a)	240	194	(a)
United States	933	1,104	1,446	1,643	1,645	1,985
TOTAL EUROPE	129	326	1,037	00	771	2,550
France	(a)	(a)	156	(a)	33	430
Germany	26	207	192	2	331	658
England	(a)	(a)	389	(a)	(a)	578
Yugoslavia	41	36	21	114	166	103
TOTAL ASIA	146	144	138	437	934	1,104
Japan	59	104	103	123	893	1,046
Philippines	15	(a)	(a)	236	(a)	(a)
TOTAL AFRICA	645	616	(a)	1,503	1,482	(a)
Zaire	227	227	(a)	472	463	(a)
Zambia	363	353	(a)	791	770	(a)
AUSTRALIA	21	21	49	200	158	101
USSR	325	325	325	1,050	1,050	1,015
WORLD TOTAL	3,028	3,266	3,227	7,488	7,840	7,686

a. Too small to be recorded
b. Included because of CIPEC membership
Source: *Yearbook*, American Bureau of Metal Statistics

in the non-Communist world. That made heavy going for the members of CIPEC's marketing efforts.

If prices continue low, question of additional funding for the copper industry becomes a major issue.

Capital Investment

To deal with the investment problem involved in providing for potential scarcities in copper, we will once again fall back on American experience. As indicated in Table 10.2, the United States produced 1.6 million tons in 1972. It is the world's largest producer of primary copper, and its largest user. In 1972 American production from domestic mines accounted for almost a fourth of total world mine output of 7,488,000 tons, and American consumption was 1,985,000 tons out of a world total of 7,686,000 tons. The country's copper mining industry has consistently been able to supply a high portion of its requirements over the years, despite decreasing ore grades, and a steady increase in demand at a compound rate of about 3.5 per cent per annum. Table 10.3 illustrates this by examining three years: 1932, the Great Depression low, and twenty and forty years later.

Estimates of future requirements indicate that output will have to be increased by over 50 per cent by 1985 and practically doubled, that is to 3.3 million tons, by the end of the century. This is a tremendous expansion and calls for large investments. It is estimated that the requirement for the first million tons would be about 4 billion dollars in 1974 dollars. The second increment would call for an additional capital outlay of something like 9 billion dollars more.

Raising capital for copper mining ventures is not an especially easy undertaking. The industry has a low ratio of success in hard rock exploration, a record of high cost development, and a long lead-time, from the date of initial investment to the final realization of profit on a continuing basis. This means that the additional capital required for the American industry is not likely to come from new enterprises. It will probably have to be met by today's leading companies, including Kennicott, Phelps Dodge and Anaconda.

These organizations have indicated that their current capital outlay to produce an additional ton before refining and smelting is around $3,500. To this must be added the additional capacity for smelting, for which they reported the cost would be between $2,000 and $3,000 a ton. In other words, there is a huge capital requirement if the industry is to produce the anticipated increments of supply, particularly under the difficult new conditions

Table 10.3 United States Copper (1,000 Short Tons)

Year	Ore grade %	From US ores		From scrap		From foreign ores and net refined imports		Total	
		Tons	%	Tons	%	Tons	%	Tons	%
1932	1.82	223	49.1	140	30.8	91	20.1	454	100
1952	0.85	932	62.2	132	8.9	428	28.9	1,483	100
1972	0.55	1,643	74.1	385	17.0	203	8.9	2,268	100

created by environmental, as well as mining health and safety legislation.

Summary

Copper will undoubtedly long continue as one of man's major materials. The four principal exporters–Chile, Peru, Zaire and Zambia have worked together for some time in the Conseil Inter-gouvernemental des Pays Exportateurs de Cuivre, CIPEC, or the Intergovernmental Council of Copper Exporting Countries. Twice in 1975 they agreed on cuts in production to try and prop up sliding prices. They had only a very small measure of success because supplies were so plentiful and demand so skimpy. Nonetheless, they agreed to keep trying.

Assuming that the cartel cannot succeed in supporting the market or make significant price increases stick, there is every reason to assume that the world's requirements for copper will be met at price levels not significantly different from those shown earlier. Some increases will have to be incurred to cover the additional costs of investments in exploration, development and installation of smelter and mine production facilities. However, these changes in price are not likely to raise the level to a point relative to aluminum and the other alternatives that would make for significant substitutions of other materials for copper.

The likelihood of scarce copper is continuously reduced by new means of doing jobs that previously called for the 'red metal'. Microwave towers for communication are one example. Communication satellites are another.

11. Lead

BY KURT BLEICKEN

Man has used lead for at least 6,000 years. The earliest uses were for figurines, coinage, water pipes, and construction by the Greek, Roman, Egyptian and Chinese cultures. It remains the fifth most important metal.

The material is a soft, grey, malleable metal with a low melting point. In studying the metals industries, lead is particularly interesting because the major uses are so clearly defined. It is therefore quite easy to construct a model of demand for the material and make tests using various assumptions as to sector demand. Table 11.1 shows the end uses of lead and the way they have changed from 1950 to 1970.

The most important fact is that about two-thirds of the lead consumed in the United States goes to the automobile and its related industries. In 1970 storage batteries used 43 per cent of the total, and gasoline additives, 21 per cent, up from 34 and 16 per cent in 1960 and 32 and 9 per cent respectively twenty years ago.

Storage batteries are virtually 100 per cent recovered and recycled. When a new battery is purchased, the dealer takes the old one and sells it to salvage merchants, who resell it or melt it down. This means that practically all the lead in batteries is recovered and made into new products. As a result, the amount of new material required for batteries is very small unless new autos are being added at a substantial rate.

The other major use of lead is in gasoline additives. In this application the material is burned off and goes off into the atmosphere. We now know that lead is harmful to humans in forms other than bullets. As a result, over the past ten years most of the dissipative uses of lead have been made illegal. For some time it has been illegal to use it for water pipes, in interior paint and it has been outlawed in most exterior paints. The new laws governing lead-based gasoline additives are intended to reduce the amounts used in gasoline by 60–5 per cent over the next five years. Unless governments drastically change their standards, the use of lead in gasoline, a fifth of the total in 1970, will be sharply reduced before the year 2000. Most of the other uses of lead, such as, solder, cable coverings, caulking, and the lead content of brass and bronze, favor reclaiming.

In addition to the outlawing of lead-based products just outlined, 'better' products, usually made of plastic or aluminum are replacing it. Solder used to connect copper pipes is slowly giving way to plastic adhesives used with tubing. Lead sheathing for underground electrical cables has been cut by 60 per cent

Table 11.1   United States End Use Consumption of Lead
1950–1970 (1,000 Short Tons)

	1950	1960	1970
Metal Products			
Storage batteries	398	353	593
Solder	95	60	70
Cable coverings	132	60	51
Caulking lead	53	67	35
Brass and bronze	24	21	19
Other metal products	212	162	192
TOTAL	914	723	961
Dissipative Uses			
Gasoline additives	114	164	279
Other	210	134	119
TOTAL NET END USE CONSUMPTION	1,238	1,021	1,360

PERCENTAGE OF TOTAL NET END USE CONSUMPTION

	1950	1960	1970
Metal Products			
Storage batteries	32	34	43
Solder	8	6	5
Cable coverings	11	6	4
Caulking lead	4	7	3
Brass and bronze	2	2	1
Other metal products	17	16	14
TOTAL	74	71	70
Dissipative Uses			
Gasoline additives	9	16	21
Other	17	13	9
TOTAL NET END USE CONSUMPTION	100	100	100

Source: United States Bureau of Mines *Minerals Yearbook*

from 1950–70 as 'better' plastics and aluminum products have replaced the earlier lead ones. Quotes are put around the word 'better' since this may mean very different things. It may mean cheaper, as in the case of plastic piping, which is less expensive than copper and involves less labor in installation or, it may mean better in the sense of lower costs, better performance, greater longevity, or more attractive appearance. Caulking lead, used around soil pipes in plumbing, is being replaced by a plastic soil pipe which is glued by plastic adhesives. The high price of brass and bronze products is curtailing their use in many areas. Therefore, the use of lead as an alloy for those metals is slowly declining.

The governments of most industrialized nations are legislating against the dissipative uses of lead. This will mean that a greater percentage of total consumption will be in products where the lead content can be reclaimed. This figures prominently in our projections of future lead consumption.

Lead Consumption Projections

The high, medium and low projections for future consumption made by Resources for the Future in 1963 and by the National Commission on Materials Policy United States in 1973 are shown in Figure 11.1. The RFF high projections are based on population projections no longer appropriate. Therefore, we would expect that the actual usage from 1960 to 1970 to follow the RFF low or medium projections. In fact, actual usage followed the medium projection very closely through the early 1970s, The National Commission on Materials Policy therefore seemed justified in just extending the RFF projection to the year 2000, despite the fact that legislation sharply curtailing the use of lead in gasoline was noted in the Commission's report.

The reason for the actual consumption figure following the RFF medium projections is mainly because of the rapid and unanticipated rise in the sales of snowmobiles, motorcycles, campers, and the myriad of recreational vehicles in which lead storage batteries are used for ignition, lighting and sometimes propulsion. This is the most important factor in the rise of lead consumption figures in the past few years. We have already mentioned that batteries are almost 100 per cent recovered. Throughout the 1950s the lead required in making batteries only slightly exceeded the lead recycled from the old ones. In the mid-1960s when the recreational vehicle boom began in earnest, the number of batteries purchased shot up for several years. In 1971 the lead going into new batteries was 680,000 tons, while the lead

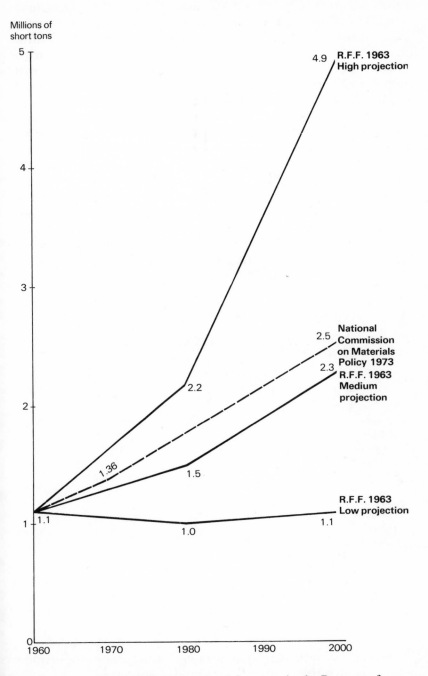

Millions of
short tons

Figure 11.1 Projections of United States Lead Consumption by Resources for
Future, 1963, and the National Commission on Materials Policy, 1973.

recovered from old batteries was only 333,000 tons. This meant that 347,000 tons more new lead was required for batteries in 1971 than was recycled. This continues as long as the number of batteries per person continues to expand. At some point, maybe now in the mid-1970s, the increasing purchases of recreational vehicles will level off (or decline), and the lead reclaimed from old batteries will again closely approximate the quantity required for new batteries. But the 1960–70 bulge in battery demand has disguised the real decline in requirements for this material in most other uses.

Recycling Lead in 1970

Before making projections of future lead requirements, let us take a close look at the current recovery of the metal from both old and new lead scrap. Table 11.2 shows the major uses for which the material is potentially recoverable and the amount actually recovered in 1970, as reported by the United States Bureau of Mines.

Table 11.2   Recovery of Old and New Lead Scrap in Relation to 1970 End Use Consumption (1,000 Tons)

	1970 Uses of Lead	Potentially Recoverable	1970 Actually Recovered
Metal Products			
Storage batteries	593	593	350
Solder	70	70	
Cable coverings	51	51	139
Caulking lead	35	35	
Other	192	119	
Brass and bronze	19	19	17
Dissipative Uses			
Gasoline additives	279	0	0
Other	119	0	0
TOTAL	1,360	888	506
Total old lead recovered			506
Total new lead scrap			91
TOTAL SECONDARY LEAD			597

As can be seen, the lead *actually recovered* (both new and old) was two-thirds of that *potentially recoverable*. This is an important ratio since, as the dissipative uses (some 29 per cent

Table 11.3 United States End Use Consumption of Lead 1950, 1960, 1970 and Projections of Demand and Recovery for 2000 (1,000 Tons)

	1950	1960	1970	PROJECTIONS FOR THE YEAR 2000			
				Total	*Potentially Recoverable*	*Projected Recovery*	*Percentage Recovered*
Metal Products							
Storage batteries	398	353	593	770	770	693	90
Solder	95	60	70	50	50		
Cable coverings	132	60	51	20	20	90	50
Caulking lead	53	67	35	10	10		
Other metal products	212	162	192	200	100		
Brass and bronze	24	21	19	25	25	23	92
TOTAL	914	723	961	1,075	975	806	83
Dissipative Uses							
Gasoline additives	114	164	279				
Other	210	134	119	50			
TOTAL END USE Consumption	1,238	1,021	1,360	1,125	975	806	72 % of total

Source: United States Bureau of Mines *Minerals Yearbook* 1950, 1960, 1970. Projections by Bleicken

of the total) are phased out, the overall recovery rate should rise. Furthermore, once we have again reached a new plateau in the number of batteries purchased, per year, *per capita*, the recovery rate from batteries should go over 90 per cent. In 1970 this would have meant a recovery rate in all *metal products* of 87 per cent instead of the actual 67 per cent.

Projected Lead Requirements for the Year 2000

Since we have good information on lead use and recovery, we will use a somewhat detailed method of projecting demand for both new lead requirements, and total consumption. The recent history of American lead consumption and a reasonable outlook for the year 2000 are presented in Table 11.3.

To arrive at the projections the following assumptions were made:

1. Storage battery uses increase in line with population.
2. Solder consumption declines slightly in line with past twenty years experience.
3. Lead cable coverings continue to lose ground to plastic or aluminum substitutes.
4. Caulking lead loses to plastic substitutes.
5. Brass and bronze use increases with population.
6. Dissipative use in gasoline ends and other dissipative uses decline.

The impact of these assumptions is startling. Although the total *end use* in the year 2000 is in the same range as it has been for the last twenty years, the requirement for *new metal* drops from 763,000 tons in 1970 to 229,000 tons in the year 2000, as shown in Table 11.4.

Table 11.4   Sources of Lead, 1950, 1960, 1970 and Projections for the Year 2000 (1,000 Tons)

	1950	1960	1970	2000
Old scrap	474	465	506	806
New scrap	—	—	91	90
New lead	764	556	763	229
TOTAL	1,238	1,021	1,360	1,125

Let us assume that by the year 2000 the nation's automobile industry has produced a viable electric car, but no substitute for the lead storage battery has been developed; further, that one-third of all cars produced at that time are electric (about 3 million cars per year) and each car requires twenty storage batteries containing 20 pounds of lead. At first glance, this looks like the salvation of the lead industry. Look back at Table 11.1. It indicates that apart from a surge of 600,000 tons of new lead requirements in a space of ten years, the inventory effect takes over and there is virtually no change in the new lead requirements. The projection in Table 11.3 will be sensitive to a marked change in the dissipative uses of lead. If the scientific evidence against lead being toxic in the atmosphere or in paints changes dramatically, of if new non-harmful, but dissipative uses for lead appear, then the projection will be way off base.

Future Supply and Projected Demand

Using the previous projection, a steady decline in the demand for new lead in the United States should be expected with occasional bursts upward if the electric car, for example, or a new rash of recreational vehicles develop. United States requirements for new lead over the next twenty to twenty-five years would be on the order of 12 million tons of new lead, give or take a few million tons. This compares to the Bureau of Mines and the National Commission on Materials Policy estimate of cumulative American lead demand of 34 million tons. American reserves of lead, mineable at current prices, amount to 39 million tons, according to the United States Geological Survey. It would appear, therefore, that the United States has enough lead to supply its own needs at current prices for around seventy-five years. Needless to say, the country's lead reserves at higher prices would be much larger than these figures would indicate.

Currently the United States is importing about a fifth of its needs, from Canada (30%), Peru (22%), Australia (21%), Mexico (10%) and other countries (17%). Within the next few years, as the laws reducing the dissipative uses of lead are more fully felt, American demand for new lead will drop quite sharply. If this occurs during the same time that American lead production is near 670,000 tons per year, it is conceivable that the United States could have an exportable surplus.

As shown in Figure 11.2, there has been a steady and rapid growth of lead production all over the world since the Second World War. The expansion since 1960 is especially noteworthy. Since most of the industrialized nations have outlawed lead in paints, set emission controls on lead oxide levels coming from smelters, and are seeing the same kind of substitution of plastics

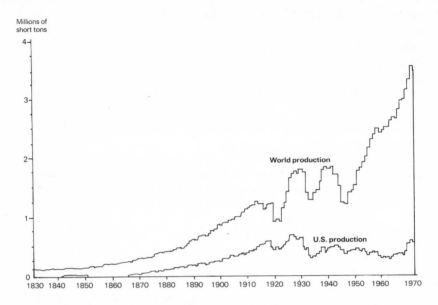

Figure 11.2   Production of Primary Lead in the World and in the United States. Source: Geological Survey Professional Paper 820, p. 316

and aluminum for lead, the question is 'who is using all the lead?'

Past American experience suggests that much of it is going into batteries for the world-wide expansion in the use of automobiles, trucks, tractors, motorcycles, boats and other motor powered vehicles. Will the world-wide growth pattern of lead consumption slow down? If the rest of the world comes anywhere near the United States in use of motorized vehicles over the next twenty-five years, the growth of world demand may continue upward. While it is likely that the more mature industrialized countries will be in a pattern of stable consumption, expansion in the rest of the world can easily take up the slack.

Current world reserves of lead are estimated to be 140 million tons. This would be about a twenty-five to thirty years supply at current prices. However, *United States Mineral Resources* estimates a potential world total of 1.5 billion tons. Included in this figure are some futuristic estimates for lead resources in underwater manganese nodules, which may be uneconomic for some time. However, a great deal of lead will move over to the 'measured and indicated reserves' column if the price increases, or as new mining techniques lower the grade of ore necessary for economic extraction. In brief, it seems unlikely that the physical supply of lead will be a problem until well past the year 2000.

On the other side of the coin there is always the possibility of a new type of electric storage battery being developed which will not use lead. Such research is now being conducted on a number of power cells like those used in space. These include lightweight sodium-sulfur batteries, and lithium-water batteries. If the demand for an electric car becomes widespread, development programs in these areas will surely be funded more generously since the weight difference between such power sources and lead-acid batteries could be 300–500 pounds per vehicle. Needless to say, such a development could throw all present-day projections for future demand for lead out of the window.

12. Ferroalloys

By Kurt Bleicken

Although steel is number one amongst the metals, it is the ferro-alloys that make special steels that are tough, stainless, heat resistant and malleable. These are the characteristics of the alloy steels which are vital to milk cans, machine tools, turbine engine blades and the other machinery, equipment and accessories essential for today's industrial world.

To make these materials, in some cases, the alloying element or its ore is combined with iron in a smelter to produce the ferroalloy to be used in making steel. In other cases, either the pure ferroalloy metal or its ore is used directly in the steel-making process. Alloying elements such as copper and molybdenum that do not oxidize too readily can be added to the charge that goes into the furnace prior to melting. Materials such as chromium and manganese that oxidize more readily are added towards the end of the refining process. Elements such as aluminum, boron, titanium and vanadium that oxidize easily are added when the melt is in the ladle.

Steels that contain one or more added alloying elements are called alloy steels. They are used in applications where hardness or toughness of carbon steel is insufficient, or in objects that would crack if hardened by the quench method used for carbon steel, or when the extra hardness and strength of alloy steels are required. Axles, bearings, forging dies and gears are typical of the products requiring extra strength and hardness.

While most people know that there are such things as ferro-alloys or alloy steels, few understand how big an industry it is in comparison with the other metals producers. Table 12.1 shows the relative importance of the major metals in terms of tonnage and value of output in 1973.

In terms of quantity the ferroalloy industry is the third largest of the American metals group. In dollar value, it is about the same size as the lead and zinc industries.

Table 12.1   Relative Size of the United States Metals
Industries 1973)

	Tons	*Approximate Total Value ($)*
Steel	168,000,000	28,000,000,000
Aluminum	6,600,000	3,000,000,000
Ferroalloys	2,900,000	614,000,000
Copper	2,350,000	2,800,000,000
Zinc	1,490,000	641,000,000
Lead	1,485,000	502,000,000

Importance of the Steel Industry to the Ferroalloys

While the steel industry could not function without the ferroalloys, the various alloy materials would not be of much importance without the steel makers. In fact, the greatest percentage
of the alloy metals consumed goes directly to steel making as
shown in Table 12.2.

Table 12.2   Importance of the
Steel Industry to the
Additive or Alloy
Metals

	Percentage Consumed by the Steel Industry
Chromium	67
Manganese	90
Molybdenum	90
Nickel	80
Silicon	90
Vanadium	80

Obviously the future of these alloy metals is very closely tied
to that of the steel industry. Since iron is a hugely abundant
element in the earth's crust and the subject of numerous reports,
we have not considered it desirable to make an analysis of the
iron and steel industry here.

As is clear from Table 12.3, the world has enough iron ore
in *reserve* to last over 100 years, and enough in *identified resources*

for another 100, 200 or more years at current rates of consumption. World consumption is growing, but even at the current growth rate it is difficult to see any chance of depletion problems in the coming centuries.

Table 12.3 World Iron-ore Resources (Billions of Metric Tons, Figures Rounded)

Country, Region or Continent	Reserves[1]	Identified Resources[2] including Reserves
United States	9	101
North America, exclusive of United States (mostly Canada)	36	126
South America	34	94
Europe	21	34
Africa	7	31
Australia and New Zealand	17	17[3]
Asia	17	72
USSR	111	304
TOTAL	252	779

1. Reserves: Identified deposits from which minerals can be extracted profitably with existing technology and under p esent economic conditions.
2. Identified Resources: Specific, identified mineral deposits that may or may not be evaluated as to extent and grade, and whose contained minerals may or may not be profitably recoverable with existing technology and economic conditions.
3. Mostly high-grade ores: vastly greater quantities or lower grade iron formations are known but have not been assessed.
Source: United States Mineral Resources Geological Survey Professional Paper 820, 1970

In attempting to ascertain the future requirements for ferroalloys we must, within very broad limits, be able to project the size of the steel industry in whatever country is being considered. In most of the metals it is rather easy to project future national requirements for input materials. However, when the basic resources are both produced in the country and imported, it is difficult to forecast where the material will originate. That is, will it come from internal sources or foreign ones? In the case of the ferroalloys, using the United States as an illustration, larger imports of alloy steel would translate directly into a lower requirement of ferroalloys, either imported or produced in the country. In other words, even if the United States consumes more steel in the future, if a substantial part of the alloy steels are imported, then the American requirement for ferroalloy materials will not increase.

It is not our purpose to examine these problems, so we will accept the projections made by the National Commission on Materials Policy and Resources for the Future for United States steel production in the years ahead as a means for testing the resource availability of the ferroalloys for American production. These projections tacitly assume no major change in the pattern of imports and, consequently, will serve quite well as an upper limit test case.

Percentage of Ferroalloys used in Steel-making

Before discussing the projections, we must consider the use of them in relationship to the steel industry. In the past fifty years the percentage of ferroalloys in total steel-making materials has slowly increased from 1.8 per cent to between 2.3 and 2.4 per cent. This is because the American economy has required more and more special steels in each passing decade. We expect that this trend will continue and by the year 2000 ferroalloys will comprise around 2.5 per cent of total steel input.

The Resources for the Future and National Commission on Material Policy projections are shown in Figure 12.1. Discarding the RFF high projections for reasons of population assumptions which are no longer appropriate, we are left with an average low projection from both sources of about 150 million tons of metal and an average high projection of about 290 million tons. If ferroalloys comprise 2.5 per cent of steel production, this would mean ferroalloy requirements of between 3.5 million and 7.3 million tons, up from about three million tons in 1973. In other words, a growth rate of between 0.8 per cent and 1.5 per cent per year is indicated.

The Changing Mix of Ferroalloys

These aggregate numbers, although useful as a guide to overall requirements, are not specific enough to project individual alloy usage. As shown in Table 12.4 the mix of ferroalloys used in steel-making is constantly shifting.

For whatever reason the relative price of the ferroalloys, the changing end-product demand, or the invention of new or substitute alloys, the use of some alloys has increased while that of others declined. Therefore, while steel industry requirements for

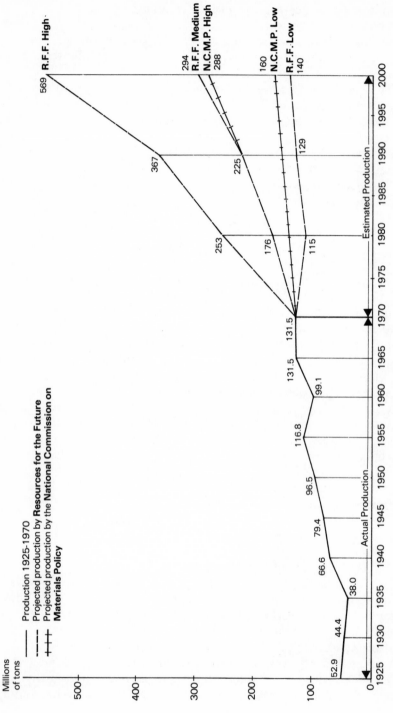

Figure 12.1 United States Steel Ingot Production. Source: United States Bureau of Mines, *Minerals Yearbook*, various years

Table 12.4 The Changing Mix of Ferroalloys (1,000 Tons)

	1950	1955	1960	1965	1970
Ferromanganese }			842	1,148	835
Silico-manganese }	720	974	101	240	193
Ferrosilicon }		382	367	595	709
Silvery Iron }	742	459	342	216	193
Chromium Alloys		408	280	384	405
Ferrotitanium	8	6	3	4	3
Ferrophosphorous	50	77	91	127	164
Other	348	106	89	91	86

Source: United States Bureau of Mines, *Minerals Yearbook* (various years)

ferroalloys have grown from 0.8 per cent to 1.5 per cent per year, the requirements for one particular ferroalloy may increase at a much faster rate than ones whose relative importance will decline.

Substitution and Relative Price of the Ferroalloys

Various sources frequently stress the fact that different ferroalloys can be substituted for one another. While this is generally true in the physical sense, it is important to realize that, in many cases, the substitution is prevented by cost differences. There are startling variations in the prices of the ferroalloys as evidenced in Table 12.5.

Table 12.5 Relative Prices of Ferroalloys (1970)

	Per Ton ($)
Ferromolybdenum	2,922
Ferrovanadium	2,583
Ferrotitanium	1,087
Ferrochromium	398
Ferrosilicon	229
Silicomanganese	195
Ferromanganese	168
Silvery Iron	91
Ferrophosphorous	40

Source: United States Bureau of Mines, *1971 Minerals Yearbook*

Thus, while ferromolybdenum may be an acceptable substitute for ferrochromium, and other ferroalloys in a physical sense, it is evident that in many cases price and other considerations would prevent free interchangeability.

Future Supply of the Major Ferroalloys

Current and future situations for each of the six leading ferroalloys, chromium, manganese, molybdenum, nickel, silicon and vanadium are briefly summarized here to give an idea of the major ferroalloy metals in terms of production and reserve relationships.

Manganese

Manganese is probably the most critical of the ferroalloys to the steel industry. To date, no substitute for this material has been found. It is used both as a scavenger to remove oxygen and sulphur from molten steel, and as an alloy to make steel shock and abrasion resistant. Most of the manganese going into the steel-making process ends up in the slag heap as a waste product where it is non-recoverable at the present time.

In the United States, there was no production of manganese ore, concentrates, or nodules containing 35 or more per cent manganese in 1973, according to the United States Bureau of Mines. Ferruginous manganese was produced in New Mexico and shipments continued from the Cuyuna Range of Minnesota. For all practical purposes, however, there is no domestic production.

In 1973, the United States consumed about one-sixth of the world's output of manganese. The country imported practically all of its supplies, 70 per cent as ore, the balance as ferromanganese. Gabon and Brazil account for more than half of the entries of ore and Zaire, South Africa, Australia, Mexico and Ghana most of the balance. Ferromanganese imports have been rising rapidly for two reasons: First, pollution problems associated with some American production; and second, Brazil, India, South Africa and some other countries want to do additional processing in their own facilities.

World reserves of manganese are very large, particularly when we consider that even the 1974 world production rates of 25 million tons a year represent only 1/260 of the current world reserves. When an economic means of mining manganese nodules from the ocean floor is developed, there could easily be an oversupply of the metal. Extensive deposits are known to exist in the Pacific, Atlantic and Indian Oceans. Recovery technology is believed feasible and both the United States and some other countries are engaged in experimental recovery. There appears to be a possibility of commercial production in the 1980s.

Table 12.6 shows 1973 mine production and reserves of manganese ore.

Table 12.6   World Prodiction and Reserves of Manganese Ore, 1973 Millions of Tons

	Mine Production	Reserves
United States	0	0
Australia	1.95	330
Brazil	2.40	95
Gabon	2.10	210
India	1.50	65
S. Africa	5.00	2,200
Communist countries	10.60	3,000
Other	1.45	30
TOTAL	25.00	6,000

Source: United States Bureau of Mines, Commodity Data Summaries

Molybdenum

Molybdenum is an alloy that imparts hardness, wear resistance and corrosion resistance to high temperature steels. It is used in making stainless steel, construction materials and special alloys. These uses makes it very important to all highly industrialized nations.

The United States supplies 60 per cent of the world's molybdenum and is the major exporter. World production of molybdenum, some 80,000 tons, is about one sixty-eighth of the currently known world reserves. There are also large identified resources of over 32 million tons, mineable at higher prices. World production and reserves of molybdenum are shown in Table 12.7.

Chromium

The three major uses of chromium are:

1. As a metal in the production of corrosion resistant stainless steels and other alloys (64 per cent).

2. As a chemical in (i) platings for steel and other metals, (ii) paints and (iii) tanning, which together with paints and chemicals accounts for 16 per cent.
3. For refractory bricks which do not melt at high temperatures are used chiefly as a lining for steel furnaces (20 per cent).

Table 12.7 Table Production and Reserves of Molybdenum Ore, 1973 (Tons)

	Mine Production	Reserves
United States	57,500	4,000,000
Canada	16,250	500,000
Chile	5,000	900,000
Peru	1,000	125,000
Other Free World	500	30,000
TOTAL	80,250	5,500,000

Source: United States Bureau of Mines, *Minerals Yearbook*, 1974

Strong demand for basic steel, stainless steel and tool steel in the early 1970s made for a sharp increase in chromium consumption. This, in the face of a shift in basic steel-making to the more efficient oxygen process which sharply reduces the demand for chrome refractories. The secondary refining or post-furnace treatment techniques involving oxygen-argon or oxygen injection in separate closed vessels have been adopted rapidly by many of the larger stainless steel melters in Europe, Japan and the United States. This permits higher production rates from furnaces and greater utilization of high-carbon ferrochromium, effecting savings estimated at $20 per ton. In 1973 the United States consumed about 20 per cent of the world's output.

Proven reserves of metallurgical grade ores are found chiefly in the USSR, Rhodesia and Turkey. Chemical grade is identified to South Africa and refractory ores to the Philippines.

In the United States chromium ore is processed into ferrochromium for metallurgical use. Although much of this processing had been performed domestically, economic and environmental reasons have shifted some of the processing overseas.

Large quantities of chromium-bearing materials are available in the United States but they are not economic under current or foreseeable conditions. In 1973, for example, the country imported 70 per cent of its requirements, 20 per cent came from sales of material declared surplus to strategic stockpile needs, and 10 per cent was derived from secondary sources. That year the imports originated in South Africa (31 per cent), USSR (21 per cent), Rhodesia (13 per cent), and Turkey and the Philippines 11 per cent each. South Africa and Rhodesia account for two-thirds of American imports of ferrochromium (Table 12.8).

Table 12.8 Major World Chromite Reserves and Production (Millions of Tons)

	Annual Production	*Reserves*
Brazil	—	6.1
Republic of South Africa	1.7	1,050
Rhodesia	0.6	550
USSR	2.1	21
Turkey	0.6	5
Finland	—	10
India	—	7
Philippines	0.6	4.7
Malagasy	—	5
Other	1.7	. 3.6
TOTAL	7.3	1,663

Source: United States Mineral Resources, United State Geological Survey, Report 820

Nickel

Nickel is used in super alloys, nickel-copper alloys, nickel alloys, cast iron, and a broad range of other applications. This makes it vital in a modern industrialized society. Over 80 per cent of the material goes into the steel industry.

In 1973 world consumption of nickel was 900,000 short tons, of which the United States share was about a third. World production is concentrated in Canada (37 per cent), the USSR (21 per cent) and New Caledonia (16 per cent). American output of nickel ore amounts to less than 10 per cent of its consumption and recovery from scrap provides an additional 30 per cent. The

United States obtains the rest of its requirements from foreign sources, namely Canada (76 per cent), Norway (8 per cent) and other countries (16 per cent).

The American Government is not now maintaining a strategic stockpile of nickel. With 76 per cent of its supply coming from Canada, the United States relies on a past history of good relationships and the many trade ties with her northern neighbor for a continued source of supply. Reserves and production are both quite widely spread so that a supply problem with any one source might be resolved by finding another one, as well as in substitutes made from other materials.

Silicon

Silicon is the second most abundant element in the earth's crust and constitutes about a quarter of it by weight. In the steel industry it is used in the form of an iron-silicon alloy, ferrosilicon, which is produced from a mixture of sand, coke and iron oxide heated in an electric furnace. When combined with steel, the material frequently is used in armatures, electromagnets, generators, relays and transformers.

Since formations as well as deposits of the material are abundant all over the world, no industrialized nation is likely to have a problem in filling its requirements.

Vanadium

Vanadium deposits occur widely, most often as a co-product with other commercial mineral deposits in which uranium and vanadium frequently are found together. For this reason, the present search for uranium will inevitably mean a substantial increase in availability of vanadium.

American consumption currently runs 20–5 per cent of the world total. In recent years the United States demand for the material has expanded sharply and is expected to increase at 5 per cent per annum into the 1980s. Domestic reserves are large. World reserves, although difficult to recover in many cases, are estimated to be adequate until well into the twenty-first century. Present mining is impeded by high cost and inefficient recovery processes. Technological improvements here are most likely, especially as much of the mineral is a co-product of the search for uranium.

Over 80 per cent of the supply of vanadium is used as an alloy for steel to improve strength, particularly high-strength low-alloy steel used in high-pressure pipes and for other construction purposes. It also has some application in titanium-based alloys for heat resistant and aerospace high-strength requirements.

Current world consumption at 18,000 tons a year is less than a five-hundredth of world known reserves. However, this can be a bit misleading in that about 85 per cent of the vanadium processed is a by-product of iron ore production, petroleum refining and the Bayer process for aluminum.

Six Ferroalloys Summary

World production, reserves, conditionally available resources, and hypothetical and speculative sources of the major ferroalloys are shown in Table 12.9.

Table 12.9   Salient Ferroalloy Statistics, 1973 (Tons)

Material	World Production	World Reserves	Conditional Resources	Hypothetical and Speculative Resources
Chromite[1]	7,300,000	1.7 billion	2.7 billion	3.6 billion
Manganese[2]	25,000,000	6.5 billion	7.7 billion	10 billion
Molybdenum	80,250	5.5 million	31.6 million	1.1 billion
Nickel	757,000	4.9 million	84 million	16 billion
Silicon	1,990,000	(3)	(3)	(3)
Vanadium	18,000	10 million	(4)	(4)

1. Chromite ore with 22–38 per cent chromium content.
2. Manganese ore with 35–54 per cent manganese content.
3. Reserves and resources are abundant and virtually inexhaustible; figures not available.
4. Vanadium resources are very large but not necessarily recoverable as it is largely produced as a by-product of other metal mining.
Source: United States Bureau of Mine Commodities Data Summary 1974 and *United States Mineral Resources* Geological Survey Paper 820, United States Government Printing Office, Washington DC

A quick glance at the millions in the annual production figures compared to the billions used to measure proven world reserves of chromium, manganese and silicon provide the first indication of availability. When we look at the thousands in calculating the world's annual output of molybdenum, nickel and vanadium it is clear that proven reserves measured in millions and potential ones in billions of tons indicate adequate physical resources.

However, the locations of producers and consumers are not identical, with the exception of silicon. Since political philosophies differ in Rhodesia, the Union of South Africa, the USSR, Japan, Europe, the United States, and many other countries, the continuation of supplies at acceptable prices is highly dependent on 'satisfactory' trade relationships.

13. Fertilizer

By Stanley A. Hutchins and
W. E. Depuy, Jr

In any discussion of world scarcity, sooner or later the focus
is on the problem of food, and its production and availability
in relation to the increasing population of the world. At times,
the food problem has been shadowed by immediate shortages
of crisis proportion, such as the results of the Arab oil embargo.
But the problem of feeding the world's population always comes
back, to hit us a little harder than it did the time before. Nations
of starving people, Bangladesh, Ethiopia, India, and others, in
newspapers and on television screens are a continuing reminder
that even the words 'shortage' and 'scarcity' become meaningless
unless people are fed.

Production of food is based on a number of controllable and
uncontrollable factors. The uncontrollable factors are those acts
of nature which disrupt our efforts to produce the needed food,
such as floods, earthquakes, drought and pestilence. Over disasters of that kind we *currently* have little or no control. However,
we do have control over a number of factors such as education
and information about food production techniques, the use of
fertilizers, seeds, soil use and care, and the end to which we
direct these means, that is the number of mouths to be fed
or population control.

Fertilizer: Organic and Chemical

Here we will deal with only one of the controllable factors: world
production and use of fertilizers. There are basically two types
of fertilizer, organic and chemical. The organic fertilizer can
be in the form of either plant or animal material which, when
combined with existing soil, aid in its enrichment. Common
examples are human and animal waste, that is, manure and,
on the plant side, 'green manure' such as soy beans, clover,
peas, alfalfa and other legumes which, when plowed under, return
vital nutrients to depleted soils. Chemical fertilizers are a basic

mixture of three ingredients found in the soil: nitrogen, phosphorous, and potassium. Depending on the degree of depletion
of the soil, chemical fetilizers are added in various combinations
to establish an optimum mix of nutrients to increase productivity.

Organic fertilizer has been employed for millennia to enhance
crop yields. Manure has been used ever since farmers discovered
that a liberal dose of either human or animal excreta made crops
healthier, faster growing, and more abundant. Other plant materials like wood ash and compost were used when they thought
it enhanced the effectiveness of the manure. The reason for their
discoveries was that as the organic material decomposed it supported bacteria, fungi, and other organisms which aided in bringing insoluble soil minerals into solution which in turn provided
the needed chemical balance for good crop growth.

For a long time, however, this organic process of fertilization
was essentially a hit or miss proposition, in that the exact nature
of what the fertilizers were doing to the soil was not really under-
stood. For instance, application of manures alone do not meet
the soil's requirements for balanced plant growth. Adding bones
to manure produced a greater response from crops, because bones
provide phosphorous, an essential plant nutrient which manure
lacks.

Slowly, but steadily, the chemical requirements of plants for
sustained and healthy growth were studied and became known*.
Today, fertilizer content and mixology is a highly refined science,
but still revolves around the three basic ingredients: nitrogen,
potassium, and phosphorous.

Nitrogen, Potassium, Phosphorous

It may be appropriate to give a brief description of each of
these key ingredients, their relative importance in the mix, their
characteristics, and the means and problems of their production.

Nitrogen is the most important of the three. It is found both
in the air and in the soil. Depending on location, an acre of
land contains from more than 7,000 to less than 1,500 pounds
of nitrogen. The air above each acre contains approximately 70
million pounds of nitrogen. However there is a problem. Only
certain types of plants, *legumes*, can naturally extract nitrogen
from the air and soil and put it to good use. All other forms

---

*Around 1840, the Baron Justus von Liebig, a German chemist, first explained the
nature of plant nutrition. He was able to show that certain materials increased crop
growth because they contained nitrogen, phosphorous, potassium, calcium and other
nutrients in forms which the plants could readily ingest. On the basis of this and
ensuing scientific expositions on the subject of plant growth, fertilizer was on its way
to becoming a major world industry.

of plant life are not as efficient as the legume and can easily suffer from a lack of nitrogen, owing to depletion of nitrogen from the soil or a basic inability to synthesize sufficient quantities of nitrogen from the air.

So it is not the supply of nitrogen, *per se*, which is the problem; it is converting it to more useful forms. For instance plants greedily accept nitrogen when it is combined with oxygen, or hydrogen forming nitrate (NO_3), or ammonia (NH_3). Of these two, the nitrate is more susceptible to loss in that it is more easily washed or leached away, whereas the ammonia form is more tightly held by the soil particles. But here we still speak of nitrogen in its organic state changing through biological action into its ammonia and nitrate forms.

This is not where the world fertilizer problem lies. The problem is in the production of man-made synthetic ammonia and nitrate compounds. Today, most of the nitrogen for growth is produced in chemical facilities, not in the ground. As indicated, nature somewhat limited the ability of most plants to extract enough nitrogen from the air and soil to sustain constant and even growth in one place. To counteract nature's nitrogen leaching effect upon the soil, farmers have come to rely upon man-converted nitrogen compounds which can be applied to the soil to insure its productivity.

Nitrogen comprises nearly 50 per cent of the total volume of manufactured fertilizer. This is primarily in the ammonia form which demands the use of petroleum feedstocks such as natural gas to provide the hydrogen element which combines with the nitrogen to form ammonia. Herein lies a problem since natural gas is in short supply and the cost is skyrocketing in many fertilizer-producing nations. Supply and price behavior of ammonia compounds reacts accordingly.

Phosphorous is the second important ingredient in the fertilizer triad. Except for nitrogen, unsatisfactory plant growth is more often owing to a shortage of this element than any other. Phosphorous in fertilizers is guaranteed in the form of phosphoric oxide (P_2O_5). The known world supply of phosphorous is estimated at around 50 billion tons. It is further estimated that it is in sufficient quantity to meet requirements for more than 2,000 years.

The problem with the phosphorous content of soil is, as in nitrogen, one of extracting it from its natural state and converting it to a readily acceptable nutrient. On the average there is about one-half the amount of phosphorous in the soil as there is nitrogen. But native soil phosphorous, in most instances, like nitrogen, is 'bound' or 'fixed' in very insoluble forms so that only a very small part of the total supply becomes available in any one growing season. For this reason, even though soils have a high total phosphorous content they often fail to provide available supplies adequate for maximum crop production.

Phosphate materials used in fertilizers are derived from raw rock phosphate which is mined, washed and ground. The ground rock phosphate is treated with sulphuric acid to produce what is called 20 per cent superphosphate. Concentrated superphosphate containing 42–50 per cent available phosphoric oxide (P_2O_5) is produced either by the electrical or wet chemical method.

Although the resource is there in plentiful supply, the industry's extraction capacity has not kept up with the demand. Phosphate mines have been plagued with equipment breakdowns, wrecked maintenance schedules, and so forth, because of their attempt to operate at full capacity on a non-stop basis. In a nutshell, the phosphate mining industry has not kept pace with fertilizer demand; their equipment is not sufficient in numbers or in quality and consequently they cannot meet the demand.

Potassium is the third important element in fertilizer compounds, and is guaranteed in the form of *potash* (K_2O). Most soils in the United States, for example, are far richer in potassium than in nitrogen or phosphorous. They frequently have up to 40,000 pounds of potash per acre stored within the plow depth. But like its other two counterparts, most of the potassium is locked up in the soil in forms that plants cannot readily use.

Potash itself is not in short supply; there are enough deposits around the world to meet the demand for many generations to come. But there is not a sufficient production capacity to meet the demand. Like the phosphate mining industry, the potash producers are also suffering from old age. There are no new major efforts to extract this resource from the earth, only a reliance upon the established deposits. For instance, miners and refiners in North America were operating in 1974 at or near practical capacity. However, even though price levels for their product increased substantially, there were no new production facilities announced for 1975.

This brief examination of the characteristics of the three major components of manufactured fertilizer illustrates definite similarities and differences between them. One similarity which stands out is that nitrogen, potassium, and phosphorous in their natural states are abundant. Another is that plants, in general, have a difficult time absorbing these nutrients in their natural state. These materials must be made more serviceable and this requires their industrial conversion. Both potassium and phosphorous, being minerals which are mined from the ground, are subject to the efficiency of the mining industry. This means measurements in terms of numbers of production facilities, exploration, quantity and quality of machinery, maintenance schedules, investment in new plants and machinery, productivity and so on. It is not a complicated problem but it requires two things, capital and realistic management. The resources are there; what is necessary is an efficient method of removing them from the ground in sufficient quantities to meet the world's fertilizer demands.

Nitrogen, on the other hand, is a different story. The present state of the art requires petroleum feedstocks to convert the nitrogen into its most effective fertilizer form, ammonia. That makes the industry dependent on the availability and cost of these feedstocks. Currently, natural gas is in short supply and extremely costly, thus severely affecting the nitrogen fertilizer industry.

What has been described so far is not scarcity but bad management. This is a solvable problem and the following is a discussion of what is being done about it in terms of world fertilizer production, with particular regard to the industry itself and to related factors which have a direct impact on production capacity.

Production, Consumption and Trade

In 1974 the Tennessee Valley Authority published a study entitled *World Fertilizer Market Review and Outlook*. From it a number of interesting factors emerge which help to explain the current fertilizer predicament.

1. The primary sources of world trade, North America, Western Europe, and Japan, have added very little nitrogen and phosphate capacity in recent years; yet, indigenous demand has increased in these areas, leaving less product available for export.
2. Shortages of feedstock, natural gas, naptha and other petroleum-derived feedstocks, and tight pollution standards have reduced levels of operation at many plants.
3. Increased use of urea and, in Japan, Europe, and the USSR, other nitrogen compounds for animal feed supplement has decreased the nitrogen fertilizer supply for general crop application.
4. Planned expansion in developing countries has not come on-stream as rapidly as announced. Also, some plants are operating

at lower-than-expected rates because of feedstock shortages, power failures, lack of preventive maintenance, shortages of spare parts, lack of trained manpower, and so on.

World potash capacity seems adequate to meet the demand running out to the 1980s. However the TVA cites examples for phosphate and nitrogen capacities which are rather interesting:

1. For phosphate, United States phosphate rock prices have doubled, Moroccan rock prices have tripled. Reasons cited are increased demand, lack of capacity, capital required for mine expansion, and ecological and power source constraints.
2. For nitrogen, the present world shortage is more a result of unavailability of naptha, lags in completion of plants, plants operating at less than capacity, and a shortage of fuel for transportation, with all these factors occuring during a period of high demand.

The TVA report goes on to say, in regard to ammonia production for nitrogen fertilizers, that only a fraction of total world use of natural gas is for ammonia production. In the United States in 1972 about 456 billion cubic feet of gas were used for ammonia out of a total production of 22 trillion cubic feet (approximately 2 per cent of the total!). Present estimated world reserves of gas are 2,033,372 billion cubic feet. Simply put, the fertilizer problem in the years ahead reflects a lack of *planning* and *investment*, rather than a lack of the basic resources required.

If we take a look at some of the numbers which are currently available on fertilizer consumption, production and trade, an interesting picture emerges.

Tables 13.1–13.3 provide statistics for nitrogen, phosphate, and potash in the 1972–3 time frame. If one aggregates these tables, world production of the three primary plant nutrients totaled about 82 million metric tons in 1972–3. Consumption totaled over 77 million metric tons in the same period. Both production and consumption represented approximately a 7 per cent increase over the previous year. An examination of these tables shows a number of significant facts:

1. Of the top ten producers of nitrogen, nine of them are included in the top ten consumers; five are included in the top ten importer category and five are in the top ten exporters.
2. Of the top ten producers of phosphate, eight of them are major consumers; only four are major importers and six are in the top ten of exporters.

Table 13.1 Nitrogen (N) Production, Consumption and Foreign Trade by Leading Countries, 1972–3

Country	PRODUCTION Metric Tons	PRODUCTION Rank	IMPORTS Metric Tons	IMPORTS Rank	EXPORTS Metric Tons	EXPORTS Rank	CONSUMPTION Metric Tons	CONSUMPTION Rank
United States	8,472,000	1	810,000	2	1,198,000	2	7,564,774	1
USSR	6,551,000	2	13,400*	—	217,800	1	5,624,000	2
Japan	2,454,100	3	—	—	1,679,600	1	732,900	9
China	2,245,000*	4	1,248,000*	1	34,000*	—	3,459,000*	3
France	1,471,869	5	222,700	9	193,072	—	1,661,786	5
West Germany	1,470,557	6	281,938	6	451,415	5	1,189,022	6
Netherlands	1,188,489	7	27,686	—	820,362	3	375,457	—
Poland	1,147,276	8	37,366	—	337,777	8	978,875	7
India	1,051,000	9	691,375	3	—	—	1,778,000	4
Italy	1,045,519	10	86,060	—	264,877	—	691,806	10
Romania	874,000	—	—	—	429,000*	6	421,000	—
United Kingdom	816,000*	—	153,300*	—	75,300*	—	946,800*	8
Canada	800,000	—	25,000	—	385,000	7	440,000	—
Belgium	646,094	—	101,163	—	514,210	4	166,743	—
Norway	395,700	—	—	—	315,500	9	78,800	—
Mexico	356,313	—	202,081	10	48,390	—	519,320	—
Egypt	151,800	—	240,000*	8	—	—	350,000*	—
Brazil	71,038	—	323,978	5	828	—	394,188	—
Kuwait	269,549	—	—	—	276,378	10	—	—
Indonesia	59,857	—	244,907	7	—	—	347,404	—
Turkey	145,200*	—	344,000*	4	—	—	375,000*	—
WORLD TOTAL	38,028,045		7,707,459		8,142,664		36,051,641	

*Unofficial figures
Source: Annual Fertilizer Review 1973, Food and Agriculture Organization of The United Nations

Table 13.2 Phosphate (P_2O_5) Production, Consumption and Foreign Trade by Leading Countries, 1972–3

Country	PRODUCTION Metric Tons	Rank	IMPORTS Metric Tons	Rank	EXPORTS Metric Tons	Rank	CONSUMPTION Metric Tons	Rank
United States	6,554,552	1	282,000	3	1,291,000	1	4,601,224	1
USSR	2,929,000	2	104,000	7	95,300	9	2,594,000	2
France	1,611,479	3	400,739	2	111,743	8	2,058,393	3
China	1,031,000*	4	18,200*	—	5,700	—	1,043,500	4
West Germany	985,975	5	116,041	6	173,334	6	902,595	5
Australia	900,000*	6	10,000*	—	100*	—	880,000*	6
Belgium	787,728	7	53,353	—	463,171	2	148,836	—
Poland	763,040	8	12,324	—	9,500	—	781,605	7
Japan	728,900	9	16,800	—	59,800	—	717,000	8
Canada	720,000	10	65,000	—	340,000	3	445,000	—
Italy	500,049	—	155,618	5	35,216	—	583,214	—
United Kingdom	467,000	—	74,900	10	60,900*	—	469,700	—
Netherlands	351,492	—	74,104	—	297,591	4	101,001	—
India	330,000	—	211,365	4	—	—	584,000	10
Brazil	277,330	—	433,315	1	2,116	—	708,529	9
Tunisia	217,200*	—	—	—	189,100*	5	17,800*	—
Morocco	154,234	—	—	—	122,379	7	49,800*	—
Bulgaria	129,500	—	102,100*	8	—	—	230,097	—
Hungary	180,816	—	82,800*	9	1,000*	—	266,177	—
Romania	312,619	—	—	—	70,000*	10	172,900	—
WORLD TOTAL	23,687,667		3,575,632		3,934,594		22,595,435	

* Unofficial figures.
Source: Annual Fertilizer Review 1973, Food and Agriculture Organization of the United Nations

Table 13.3 Potash (K₂O) Production, Consumption and Foreign Trade by Leading Countries, 1972–73

Country	PRODUCTION Metric Tons	Rank	IMPORTS Metric Tons	Rank	EXPORTS Metric Tons	Rank	CONSUMPTION Metric Tons	Rank
USSR	5,433,000	1	—	—	1,705,600	3	3,238,000	2
Canada	3,820,000	2	50,000	—	3,810,000	1	180,000*	5
West Germany	2,497,679	3	67,115	—	1,399,925	4	1,147,546	6
East Germany	2,458,000*	4	—	—	1,820,000*	2	655,000*	1
United States	2,432,000	5	2,896,000	1	836,000	5	4,002,053	3
France	1,664,480	6	198,624	—	825,680	6	1,635,101	—
Israel	621,590	7	—	—	583,945	7	13,320	—
Spain	532,852	8	84,600*	—	216,384	8	258,839	—
China	300,000*	9	1,300*	—	—	—	375,700*	—
Congo	283,100*	10	—	—	—	—	3,500*	—
Italy	130,551	—	209,796	—	25,622	9	266,297	4
Poland	—	—	1,163,402	2	—	—	1,285,225	7
Japan	—	—	536,800	4	—	—	599,600	8
Czechoslovakia	—	—	590,000*	3	—	—	585,100*	10
United Kingdom	—	—	495,100*	5	—	—	435,100*	9
Brazil	—	—	456,412	6	—	—	456,232	—
Belgium	—	—	318,604	8	—	—	187,900	—
Hungary	—	—	345,800*	7	—	—	328,620	—
India	—	—	316,302	9	—	—	332,000	—
Netherlands	3,587	—	230,834	10	3,660	10	126,499	—
WORLD TOTAL	20,197,914		10,864,661		11,241,316		18,750,488	

* Unofficial figures
Source: Annual Fertilizer Review 1973, Food and Agriculture Organization of The United Nations

3. Of the top ten producers of potash, only five are top ten consumers; only one, the United States, is a major importer, and eight are major exporters.
4. Nitrogen and phosphate production is found in many countries, while potash is virtually limited to eleven nations with the USSR in a substantial lead position.

The Fertilizer Forecast

Table 13.4 is a forecast of world consumption of primary plant nutrients out to 1980 based on two possible levels of growth.

A projection of this sort is included in this discussion to give a general feel for what might happen if the industry begins to pick up a bit, the supply and demand levels normalize somewhat, and natural disasters do not frequent themselves upon the world growing regions. That all will progress smoothly out to 1980 is unlikely; however, both consumption and production of fertilizers will increase.

The report of the Committee on Agriculture and Forestry of the United States Senate on the *US and World Fertilizer Situation* of December 1974 includes a number of interesting projections which merit inclusion here:

1. World fertilizer consumption is expected to increase at a compound annual rate of $5\frac{1}{2}$ per cent. All three nutrients will experience a similar situation, although nitrogen should grow somewhat faster.
2. Nitrogen will be plentiful, even abundant, but the over-capacity situation should not be nearly as severe as in the 1960s.
3. Projected fertilizer use is not necessarily sufficient to meet the world's food needs in 1980.
4. Production-consumption projections for the major countries indicate an excess of fertilizer supplies, primarily in nitrogen and potash.
5. Japan will lose its place as the largest nitrogen net exporter, probably to the USSR or Netherlands.
6. The less developed countries expect to increase production by nearly 180 per cent, compared to 57 per cent in the developed countries. While they will be essentially self-sufficient in nitrogen, imports of phosphate and potash will increase somewhat.
7. The Middle East countries, provided they overcome current production problems, could become the largest world's nitrogen exporters.

Table 13.4 Total Primary Plant Nutrient Consumption (1972) Forecast by Region (1980) (Million Tons N, P$_2$O$_5$, K$_2$O)

Region	Actual Consumption 1972	CONSUMPTION FORECAST–1980			Range Variation (%)	AVERAGE ANNUAL GROWTH RATE 1972–1980 (%/year)	
		Midpoint	Low	High		Low	High
Developed							
North America	16.5	24.3	22.5	26.2	±7.6	4.1	6.0
Western Europe	17.5	22.6	21.7	23.5	±4.0	2.7	3.8
Other[a]	4.3	5.5	4.2	6.8	±23.6	—	6.2
Total	38.3	52.5	48.5	56.5	±7.6	3.0	5.0
Developing							
Latin America	3.2	7.2	6.6	7.8	±8.3	9.5	11.8
Africa[b]	1.3	2.2	1.9	2.4	±11.4	5.9	9.0
Asia[c]	5.4	10.8	9.6	11.9	±10.7	7.7	10.6
Total	9.9	20.2	18.2	22.2	±9.9	8.0	10.7
TOTAL	48.2	72.7	66.6	78.7	±8.3	4.2	6.3
Eastern Europe–USSR	18.9	32.0	30.1	33.9	±5.9	6.1	7.6
Other Asia	4.9	9.1	8.1	10.1	±11.0	6.6	9.6
WORLD	72.3	113.7	104.8	122.6	±7.8	4.8	6.9

a. Includes Japan, Israel, Republic of South Africa, and Oceania.
b. Excludes Republic of South Africa.
c. Excludes Japan and Israel.
Source: Tennessee Valley Authority. National Fertilizer Development Center, *World Fertilizer Market Review and Outlook*, Bulletin Y-70, March 1974, p. 8

The Tennessee Valley Authority report, from which Table 13.4 was extracted, also projects consumption and production of fertilizers out to 1980. According to the TVA study, total world fertilizer consumption is forecast to exceed 100 million metric tons in 1980. Average world consumption growth rate is expected to range from 4.8 to 6.9 per cent per year between 1974 and 1980. Of the developed regions, the fastest growth rates will be in Eastern Europe and the Soviet Union, 6.1–7.6 per cent annually. The average annual rate of consumption increase in developing regions will range from 8 to 10.7 per cent; Latin America is predicted to experience larger gains than either Asia or Africa. This compares with expected rates of 4 to 6 per cent in the developed regions. In developing Asian countries the consumption growth rate is expected to range between 7.7 and 10.6 per cent.

Nitrogen is projected to experience the greatest gain, increasing from 33.7 million metric tons in 1972 to 57 million metric tons in 1980. At that time, nearly 39 million of the 57 million metric tons will be used in the developed regions, 11 million in the developing regions and 6.8 million in the other Asian Countries. The largest user of nitrogen will be Eastern Europe, and the USSR, followed by North America, Western Europe, and the developing nations of Asia, which will increase use at an annual rate to exceed 9.4 per cent per year.

By 1980 the total world use of *phosphates* is projected to between 28 and 34 million metric tons. The annual growth rate, on the average, is forecast at about 5 per cent per year. Phosphate use is centered in the developed regions, which accounted for over 80 per cent of total use in 1972. By 1980 their share is predicted to decline to 76 per cent of the world market.

The largest consumer of phosphates is Western Europe, followed by Eastern Europe and North America; each employed well over 4 million metric tons of phosphate in 1972. The developing nations of Asia rank fourth with a consumption level just over 1.3 million metric tons. Phosphate use is projected to more than double in the developing countries, but their total use will remain only about a fourth of that of the developed regions.

By 1980, the total use of *potash* in the developing regions will be about 3 million metric tons and in the developed regions should exceed 22 million metric tons. Most of the potash trade is between developed nations. The major reserves and production facilities for potash are located in the developed countries and, therefore, the developing countries should expect to continue obtaining their potash requirements through trade. The only region currently planning any major expansion of their potash capacity is Eastern Europe, including the Soviet Union. This increased capacity will place them at the forefront of the world's potash producers.

Summary

Since fertilizer is so often referred to as one of the world's rapidly developing scarce resources it has to be included in *A World of Scarcities*. Hopefully the discussion presented here will redirect the attention of those concerned with fertilizer shortages.

As far as the availability of the three main ingredients of fertilizer compounds is concerned, it is quite clear that there is no cause for alarm. Nitrogen, potassium, and phosphorous are here on earth in enough quantity to keep us fertilizing effectively for centuries.

What we have had a shortage of in this essential product, is an adequate and productive industry, one with foresight and managerial skills. This is a man-made problem and one that is readily recognized by those in the field. However, although the problem is quite clear, whether or not anything will be done remains to be seen.

Availability of fertilizer, like that of other natural resources, is a question of management and preparedness. To have the world's fertilizer industries capable of meeting current and future demands will require substantial investment in plants, equipment, and personnel; continuing and expanding research programs to produce fertilizers more cheaply and efficiently; and advanced experimentation in the application and use of fertilizer compounds.

A further necessity is experimentation in the field of organic fertilizer. The chemical side of fertilizers has been fairly well covered here, but the organic side has not. The reasons for this are two-fold. First, present-day fertilizer shortages or scarcities are in the chemical compounds, not in the organic ones. Second, animal and human excreta are certainly in no short supply; neither is the availability of 'green' manure, soy beans, clover, and other leguminous plants.

Recently, with the fertilizer industry's inability to meet the demand for their chemical product, farmers have taken another look at organic fertilizers as a means to enhance their yields. In fact, some farmers have noticed a steadily declining effectiveness in the chemical fertilizers which they have been applying, while noting increased yields and healthier crops when organic fertilizers are employed.

To meet the demand for food production into the twenty-first century, the fertilizer industry has its work cut out. Farmers must consider all the means at their disposal to effectively enhance the yields of their crops and the chemical fertilizer industry must place greater emphasis on managing itself to meet the current and future demand for its product.

Index